More Than Your Trauma

A Personal Growth Journey for Young Black Women Restoring your Inner Child & Inner Peace

Victoria Anderson

Table of Contents

Trigger Warning: The book mentions multiple traumas, self-harm, and other sensitive topics that might upset some readers.

Introduction

Dear Black woman, you are meant for more than scars from unprocessed trauma. It took generations of resilience, softness, and wisdom to make you—it's time to live like it.

In America, a limited number of people know how it feels to carry generational trauma and still be expected to thrive. We often work four times as hard to be noticed in a world that discounts our identity and marginalizes our existence. African American women are among the few who know this reality firsthand. Living our truth isn't easy in a society that belittles us and forces us to hide layers of ourselves to fit the mold. We see, feel, and carry the burdens of generations through passed-down stories, firsthand experiences, and systems perpetuated in society. We are often exposed to narratives of the African American family unit being divided and broken down. These experiences and stories program and reprogram our minds to believe that it's normal for us to stay on guard against the world. After all, we are "strong Black women," right?

The statement above is true, but we are also more than that. We Black women need to know that just because the world refuses to see us as complete doesn't mean we should succumb to existing as fragments of ourselves. Our stories are important, and we are far more than strong; we are mothers, people, lovers, daughters, sisters, and friends. We are lined with strength, but softness and wisdom are also parts of us. Our journeys are essential, and we have the right to heal from generations of brokenness. A Black woman's healing doesn't deny her history; instead, this journey embraces it. We stand on the backs and shoulders of our ancestors who fought so that we could live in spiritual, emotional, and physical freedom today; healing is our inheritance. The best part is that the power to heal is within us. Sure, it takes work, commitment, optimism, and much affirmation, but we are predestined to overcome. Our experiences of trauma—along with the lineage of hurt in our veins—do not define or minimize us.

I was raised by a single mother of two who found a way to break the cycle of trauma by escaping an abusive husband—a man I call dad. Watching the woman who brought me into this world actively fight daily traumas such as project housing, state benefits, and so on fueled me with purpose as a child; that's something I haven't truly realized until recently. My mother, a remarkable Black woman, was adamant about breaking free. She would not depend on anyone or be deterred by anything in her life's journey. I like to believe those same traits have been passed down to me. If trauma can be passed down through generations, the good stuff is too.

Think of the mind as a card catalog, a reference library, or a picture archive; there's often no way to unsee, unfeel, and unknow what has happened to us. Traumatic experiences replay in our interactions, thoughts, and emotions—often in a loop. We can get temporarily lucky sometimes and lock it away or pause it for a while, but it will resurface until we can put a name to it, assign a culprit, know we aren't to blame, and consciously strip away the power it has over us. We don't want trauma to win; there's simply no room for that. We don't want it to induce long-term suffering or define us either. Instead, we want to seize victory over trauma and become whole. That victory means recognizing and reckoning with the defeated space we hold for trauma so that we can cope with it.

This book lets you deepen your understanding of yourself and use it to thrive in the world around you. Through strategies based on understanding your trauma, you can start healing it. It puts you in a position to work toward growth. It's an opportunity to remove the shame of the trauma experience and transform it for the betterment of your life. This is a chance for you to look at your deepest, most painful parts and call them worthy, loved, and capable. The book also gives you a sneak peek into interactive elements for recognizing and recovering from trauma; the companion workbook explores these more deeply.

You don't have to live in that pain anymore. Take this as permission to step away from the weight of detrimental expectations put on you. This is your chance to form a new, better reality that proves you can overcome and be transformed by your trauma.

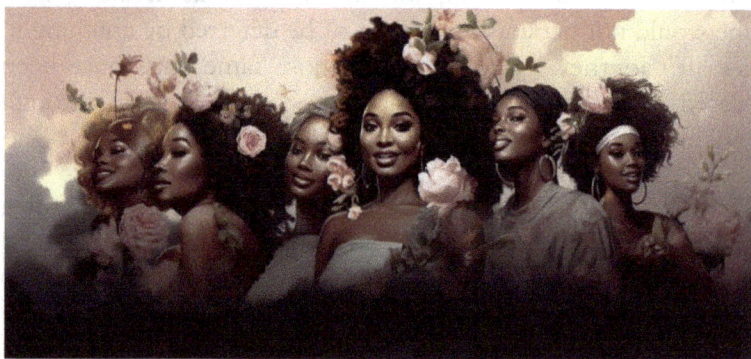

Chapter 1:

Putting the Spotlight on

Trauma—What Is It?

Bad things happen; sometimes, these are multilayered and difficult to process. The experience of bad things happening that cause long-term stress and a prolonged change in the way you view the world is trauma. A single incident can result in trauma. However, trauma can also come from continuous exposure to stress over an extended period. An incident can occur that lasts only a few seconds but changes your life forever. For example, a car accident is a form of single-incident trauma. Continuous exposure to difficult experiences such as domestic violence at home, however, is a more ongoing form of trauma.

Trauma can be described as the shock, denial, confusion, numbness, anxiety, and dissociation that are experienced during and after stressful events, making it challenging for us to cope with the demands of daily life. Any event that causes fright or distress can be considered traumatic. Trauma can affect anyone at any age and from any background, albeit in different ways. Feelings that are commonly associated with trauma include fear, powerlessness, despair, anger, depression, and guilt. Many of us experience traumatic events in our lives; some of us may be aware of what these are, but others might not be.

This chapter explores the concept and lived experience of trauma. The aim is to unpack what trauma is, the feelings associated with it, and the groups who are most vulnerable to it. The chapter also identifies the different types of trauma that individuals can experience.

Exploring Trauma

Very few people can go through life without encountering some form of trauma. Also, everyone is affected differently by traumatic experiences. Unlike normative adversity, traumatic experiences are often emotionally damaging. Everyday hardship leads to personal growth, while trauma eventually damages the connection to oneself and the rest of the world. Traumatic experiences are typically unpredictable and beyond a person's control. Trauma undermines a person's sense of security and belonging, creating the belief that danger is always around the corner. Losing a parent, retrenchment (being let go at work), sexual assault, and child neglect are just a few examples of traumatic experiences.

Even though trauma affects everyone, certain groups are more vulnerable to experiencing it than others. This is based on history, institutionalization, and the continuation of disadvantageous systems. Groups that are commonly in the crosshairs of trauma are Black, Indigenous, people of color (BIPOC), military veterans, people in prisons, refugees, asylum seekers, disabled people, the LGBTQIA+ community, and impoverished people. These groups are typically marginalized and made to question their belonging, which is a breeding ground for trauma to develop.

Caregivers are also vulnerable to experiencing trauma (Bowdler, 2023). I know this firsthand because I was a caregiver for my mom while she battled end-stage renal disease. I stayed by her side to the very end of her illness, and it was the most traumatic thing I have ever experienced to date. I genuinely believe I'll never have to go through anything as traumatic as that was. Caregiver trauma is something I'm still working through; I'm actually in therapy for it now due to PTSD from the experience.

High-stress environments and the severity of the illnesses that caregivers are exposed to can lead to a state of mental and physical exhaustion, also known as caregiver trauma. Experiences of high-demand support provision and dealing with intense illnesses can have adverse outcomes on the person providing care, such as depressive moods, anxiety, PTSD, and compassion fatigue or burnout. The caregiving experience is all-encompassing, and it affects caregivers on many levels, causing emotional and physical strain that comes from managing a patient's needs. A lack of support and readiness to provide care can add to caregiver trauma.

Common symptoms of trauma in caregivers can include excessive tiredness, physical pains, drastic appetite changes, feelings of loss or hopelessness, withdrawal from social interactions, and increased agitation. A fundamental way to prevent caregiver trauma, and any other forms of trauma, is taking care of oneself. The topic of self-care will be discussed later in the book, so stay tuned.

Some traumatic experiences are more evident than others, but there's no default experience of trauma because it's a personal journey. Examples can include one-off (a car accident) or ongoing events (domestic abuse), being directly harmed (firsthand experiences) or witnessing harm to someone else (secondary experiences), and being affected by trauma in the family or community, including trauma that has happened before you were born.

Some signs that you are experiencing trauma are characterized by feelings of shame, feeling stuck or trapped in your own life, believing you are unsafe and unsupported, agitation, and the persistent feeling of invalidation as well as marginalization.

Emotional and Physical Responses to Trauma

Traumatic experiences can cause people to feel a range of strong emotions directly after the traumatic incident. These emotions can last for a short while or persist, depending on the trauma experienced. Traumatized people can feel overwhelmed, helpless, and emotionally burdened by the difficulty of processing the experience.

Multiple types of trauma can result in physical and emotional symptoms. The physical reactions to trauma can include

- headaches

- exhaustion

- racing heart

- profuse sweating

- jumpiness

- digestive issues

- hyperarousal

- sleeplessness or too much sleep

Alternatively, the emotional responses to trauma can manifest as outbursts due to the challenge of coping with the experience. Flashbacks are a common emotional experience for people after trauma. A flashback is the experience of mentally reliving the traumatic event. Nightmares are common during this time, but other examples of emotional responses include

- numbness

- self-doubt

- shame

- guilt

- despair

- hopelessness

- irritability

- difficulty focusing

- anxiety

- depression

- sadness

- fear

- aggression and anger

- denial

The emotional and physical experiences of trauma will vary between people because our experiences affect us differently.

The Multiple Types of Trauma

Traumatic experiences are layered and can manifest as short-term and long-term disturbances in daily functioning. Knowing the multiple types of trauma can help us understand and cope with the experience overall.

Acute Trauma

Single traumatic events trigger an intense, short-lived reaction of distress and emotions commonly referred to as "acute stress." People who experience acute stress are most likely survivors of car accidents, physical assaults, or suddenly losing someone important to death.

Chronic Trauma

While acute trauma is a result of a single event, chronic trauma is from ongoing exposure to trauma. Persistent, prolonged, or repeated experiences are the foundation for chronic trauma. It develops in response to experiences such as persistent bullying, child neglect, emotional, physical, or sexual abuse, and domestic violence. Someone who is left in a traumatic environment for too long tends to develop different scars than people who experience single-event trauma. For example, overexposure to trauma can result in age regression, which is the experience of mentally retreating to a younger age due to a lack of emotional regulation. Prolonged trauma can keep you stuck at the age where you were victimized. For instance, you could be a 30-year-old woman today, but mentally, you retreat to your 12-year-old mindset when your trauma is triggered. Scars from single-trauma events, however, can show up as promiscuous or rebellious behaviors that keep you stuck in a self-sabotaging loop. Even so, due to the complexity of trauma, no one can definitively say how trauma will manifest in each person.

Complex Trauma

Now, take your understanding of chronic trauma and imagine that experience across a range of areas in life; that's where complex trauma comes into play. Complex trauma is the experience of repeated trauma from which there's usually no possibility of escape. For example, someone experiencing domestic violence might feel trapped in the situation or believe that their partner keeps tabs on them even outside of the home. Complex trauma causes hypervigilance and persistent monitoring of one's surroundings in anticipation of a threat, and this is highly exhausting.

Secondary (Vicarious) Trauma

People can also experience trauma from being exposed to another person's experience; this is called secondary or vicarious trauma. First responders, law enforcement, and people who deal with injuries are commonly susceptible to secondary trauma. The vicarious trauma experience can increase the risk of compassion fatigue, which refers to emotional avoidance in these situations in an attempt to self-preserve.

Adverse Childhood Experiences

Adverse childhood experiences (ACEs) commonly cover multiple childhood experiences that leave children exposed to trauma. ACEs can interfere with child development by causing emotional injury too early in a person's developmental process. Exposure to neglect, abuse, and adversity as a child at home can cause ACEs.

Different Experiences of Trauma

As people grow older with unresolved issues, trauma begins to impact today's experiences. People can be exposed to various traumatic events in their lifetime. The multiple experiences of trauma include childhood, collective, generational, moral injury, racial, and secondary trauma, all of which are explored next.

Childhood Trauma

Largely rooted in ACEs, childhood trauma is a massively scarring early experience. For instance, children exposed to a messy divorce between parents may grow to detest the idea of love or dismiss the idea of their being worthy of it. Traumatic experiences in childhood affect adult experiences. Typically, children who are unsupported, dismissed, or neglected during childhood carry trauma from it.

Here's an example of one survivor's story: From as young as Bea can remember until she left home at 18, she was exposed to her father's brutal violence toward her mom. Today, at 24, Bea is still learning to trust that healthy relationships exist regardless of her childhood experiences.

This story reminds me of the resilience in children and, equally, of the scars that childhood experiences leave on us. Fortunately, with the right strategies, we can work through anything.

Collective Trauma

Trauma that affects a large group of people simultaneously is known as collective trauma. Consider this a form of shared trauma where different people can understand and relate to a shared experience. For example, experiencing police brutality is a shared trauma among the African American community. Mass shootings would be another example. Anniversaries of collective trauma can lead to events such as memorials and media coverage to commemorate collective suffering.

Generational Trauma

This one is in its name: Generational trauma is an experience passed on from one generation to another. Many BIPOCs can relate to generational experiences of pain and inequity. For example, racial tensions and oppression are generational.

Past trauma impacts the mental and emotional health of present generations. However, the connection is not always as straightforward as we'd like. Some studies point to the possibility of generational trauma affecting us genetically (*Trauma*, n.d.). The trauma that settles in our bodies is then triggered in response to the environment we are born into. You may not have known that you have generational trauma until you get old enough to hear stories about slavery and other traumatic experiences endured by our community. Knowing of these experiences can be painful, but it empowers you to notice forms of mistreatment in the present.

Moral Injury

Anything that threatens your set of rules—especially when other people are impacted negatively by that thing—can be viewed as a moral injury. For example, regulations often undermine the needs of one group while satisfying the best interests of another. Consider segregation, for instance, where the whole system was unfair and oppressive toward people of color (POC) in favor of White people. Someone who believes that all races deserve to be treated with respect without any threat to their sense of belonging experiences moral injury when the system goes against this belief.

Racial Trauma

Racism refers to individual or institutional harm inflicted on the basis of race, whether unintentional, intentional, or systematic. This involves everything from someone making harsh judgments or mistreating a person based on their racial background to the racial pay gap. Trauma comes from being excluded or treated terribly in society because of your race. Essentially, racial trauma is caused by persistent experiences of racism. The term "racially motivated stress" can be used to describe the impacts of dealing with, or constantly anticipating the need to deal with, racism, and this type of trauma typically interlinks historical and generational experiences. For example, the constant experience of marginalization and being cut down because you are a Black person is a racial trauma. Many Black people are made to feel ashamed about an identity we should be proud of.

Traumatic experiences are detrimental to your well-being and mental health. However, the more you uncover your experiences and address the hidden emotions associated with your trauma, the better positioned you are to overcome them. The main agenda is to reveal what needs healing so that you can do the work to heal it.

Interactive Part 1: Understanding Your Trauma

As I recall my childhood experiences, I realize how much they affected my journey: My family—my mom, dad, brother, and me—lived in a house in the city. My dad was a war vet battling a drinking problem. Mom was a perpetual student completing her degree, raising two kids, and trying to support a reckless partner bent on self-destruction. Balancing children, a self-destructive spouse, and school is rarely smooth sailing.

Anyway, I would dream about a rabbit; it was my size in the dream. While picturing this rabbit, I dreamed that I could hear my parents arguing. My dad was yelling and waving a gun around; it was a dream, but it all felt terrifying and real. In this dream, Dad proceeded to come into my room and somehow shoot the rabbit—parts of the bunny's fur flew around the room, but there was also what I imagined as blood and brains that slid across the dresser and down the side. I know that sounds awful; and it was. I had this dream, as young as I was, which is quite traumatic to this day. Writing about it now, it is still as vivid as the first time I had it. The contrast of the baby blue dresser and rabbit and bright red brain matter looked horrible. I woke up in a panic only to find that my reality was just as threatening.

The yelling between my parents had started in the middle of the night—dishes breaking, thumping noises, and mom crying. It wasn't the first time. My brother and I had experienced this often enough to know we had to stay in our rooms, pretend like nothing was happening, and remain silent; that was the rule. But this time, things were different. When it was over, Mom packed us up, and off we went into the night, down the street, and around the corner to a relative's house. We hid out there for days until we could leave safely. The experience is etched in my mind, every detail of it, much like the dream I had that night. Traumatic events will stick with you, no matter your age.

This exercise is a chance for you to engage with the information from this chapter to understand your trauma and process your "rabbit." Hopefully, my story can help you navigate this interactive part as honestly as possible. Use the following set of prompts to explore how trauma experiences have affected you. This knowledge will come in handy in later chapters as you process your experiences and restore your peace.

What is your earliest memory of trauma?

_____

_____

_____

_____

How does your experience of trauma make you feel?

_____

_____

_____

_____

What are some emotional responses you have to trauma?

_____

_____

_____

What are some physical responses you have to trauma?

Are there any daily encounters that make you feel unsafe?

What type or types of trauma do you most identify with?

_____

_____

_____

When did you first realize that a specific situation traumatized you?

_____

_____

_____

What experience or experiences contributed to your trauma?

_____

_____

_____

_____

What do you need to feel safe enough to confide to someone about your experiences?

_____

_____

_____

Describe how trauma affects your current life experiences.

_____

_____

_____

Chapter 2:

Trauma's Personality—How Does It Affect Us?

Just as the experience of trauma is multidimensional, so is the way it affects us. When a trauma response is triggered, our bodies go through various emotions and physiological experiences some of which were touched on in the first chapter. Anxiety, depression, and post-traumatic stress disorder (PTSD) are some of the intense effects of ongoing or generational trauma. Not everyone who goes through something traumatic is guaranteed to develop these symptoms. However, you aren't weak-minded if you happen to experience those effects.

Traumatic experiences happen often and have significant, adverse effects on mental and physical health. Research suggests that trauma—and in particular, generational trauma—increases the risk of high blood pressure among African Americans (Gillespie, 2023). Discrimination and prejudice can perpetuate feelings of trauma, especially in Black communities. The constant experience of being marginalized because of your race adds a new layer of complexity around individual trauma, and the next chapter will discuss this more deeply.

How individuals experience trauma is ever-changing, and it varies between people. You might think you've found an effective way to cope with yours, but then suddenly, something can trigger a traumatic response. Recognizing the effects of trauma and acknowledging your experiences is the beginning of overcoming it. Your understanding of the multiple effects of trauma can help you on your healing journey. This chapter explores how trauma affects us, what can trigger trauma, and potential conditions that can arise from it.

The Effects of Trauma

When trauma manifests in the mind and through cognitive processes, people can experience flashbacks, panic attacks, dissociation, sleeplessness, self-neglect, substance abuse issues, and thoughts of self-harm or the act thereof. These manifestations can lead to poor emotional and physical health.

Flashbacks

Trauma can stimulate intrusive, unwanted memories, making survivors re-experience the sensations and emotions from traumatic events (Gardner, 2022). These memories can be random and vivid, to the point where survivors feel they are reliving the trauma experience. Multiple situations can trigger flashbacks, including smells, sounds, and other sensations. For example, a war veteran could experience flashbacks in response to a car backfiring loudly or the sound of a helicopter whirring above them. Everyone's triggers will be unique to their experience, causing various reactions.

Panic Attacks

In an attempt to respond to danger, the body can go into overdrive, resulting in an intense fear-based reaction, more commonly known as a panic attack. Panic attacks happen when your body's normal response to fear is exaggerated, causing you to feel overwhelmed. At this point, your body goes into shock from the fear, which can quickly manifest as

- a racing heartbeat

- feeling faint

- dizziness

- shaking

- feeling nauseated

- chest and stomach pains

- feeling too hot or cold

- feeling disconnected from your surroundings

Panic attacks can be sudden and typically last between five and twenty minutes. Panic attacks can make you feel frightened that you are losing control. You could also feel like you are going to faint from the dizziness, think you are about to experience a heart attack, or hyperventilate.

Panic attacks can happen at different moments. Some people can have a single panic attack and never experience one again, while others might have several of them in a short period. If you are someone who experiences regular panic attacks, you could notice that certain situations, activities, or places trigger that experience. For example, an African American teen could find encounters with the police so stressful that they lead to panic attacks.

Dissociation

The mind sometimes copes with stressful situations by dissociating from traumatic experiences altogether. This experience causes your body and mind to separate themselves from reality. It happens in an attempt to protect you from past and present horrors. People who experience dissociation can have gaps in memory and changes in identity. For example, it might be hard to remember personal events, items, and information. Survivors might even forget details about themselves and adopt a new identity to block out the painful experience.

This form of detachment happens when the body is under too much pressure. Occasionally, conditions can be so stressful that the very thought of the encounter or experience can bring on a dissociative attack. Dissociation can be short-term (lasting hours or days) or long-term —weeks, months, or even years; every person's experience is different (*Dissociation and Dissociative Disorders*, 2023).

Many people learn to dissociate as a way to cope with trauma, a habit that can start from a very young age. People who dissociate might

- see the world as aimless or foggy.

- feel like they are dreaming or in a simulation.

- think people are robots—even though they are aware it's not true.

- disconnect from their emotions and body.

- have uncertain boundaries.

- detach from world experiences.

Being pulled from reality can lead to a significant identity shift. This is when someone could act like a different person, and alter egos are an example. You might notice someone behave differently, speak in multiple voices, and switch from one part of their personality to another.

Sleeplessness

Trauma pushes the mind into a restless state. It's as though the body is consciously and subconsciously waiting for something terrible to happen again. Sleeplessness might make it challenging to concentrate and make healthy decisions. A variety of factors can cause sleeplessness, including

- problems and pressures associated with finances, housing, work, family, and many more aspects of life.

- flashbacks from negative experiences.

- a lack of security.

- mental and physical issues.

* stress and ongoing concerns.

This restless mental state can manifest as sleeplessness or trouble falling asleep. Even if you fall asleep, you might find it challenging to get quality rest.

Self-Neglect

Putting self-care on the back burner is neglect. It might be a sign of self-neglect when you don't meet your basic needs, such as general hygiene, eating, and safety. Low self-confidence, depression, and mental fatigue can lead to self-neglect. Someone who has difficulties adjusting to life following trauma might feel destabilized and struggle with taking care of themselves. Traumatic experiences take so much effort and energy to process that they can make it hard for you to care for yourself.

Thoughts of Self-Harm

Finding it challenging to take care of yourself depletes mental health. Once that happens, thoughts of self-harm often arise. Self-harm is when someone considers or carries through hurtful actions on themselves. In some cases, people self-harm as an outlet for difficult emotions. If painful memories and feelings come to the surface, someone could feel overwhelmed enough to hurt themselves.

Common reasons why people self-harm include

* the need to escape intrusive thoughts and memories.

* wanting to transform emotional pain into physical pain.

* as an attempt to stop feeling numb from trauma.

- to cultivate a sense of control.

Though many might not understand self-harm, it's an attempt to deal with the pain someone feels internally. It is crude, violent suffering that comes from a place of extreme psychological hurt.

Substance Abuse

Substance abuse happens when people use things such as drugs and alcohol to drown trauma-related emotions. Recreational drugs and other substances might ease strong emotions, but this is only temporary. Substances don't help the feeling of distress caused by trauma. Instead, they give momentary satisfaction that wears off after some time. Be aware that substance abuse is one of the easier traps to fall into in an attempt to subdue pain, but it is also as hard to climb out of once there.

Trauma affects everyone differently. Understanding how trauma affects you and being aware of unhelpful coping mechanisms can help prevent issues such as substance abuse and self-harm. Knowing your trauma makes it possible for you to overcome it. Therapy and trauma recovery strategies are great tools to transform trauma into healing; these are explored in later chapters.

The Body's Stress Response System

Trauma often manifests physically as headaches, aches, shaking, fatigue, sweating, issues with concentration, dizziness, and body pains. When we go through trauma or feel distressed, the body automatically releases a stress hormone known as cortisol, together with adrenalin, to prepare the body to respond to stress protectively. You will fight, flee, fawn, flop, or freeze as your body reacts to increased adrenaline and cortisol.

The body's stress response system protects you from fear and emotional triggers. The range of effects and responses is merely your body's attempt to survive the experience. Here's a quick note on how the body is wired to respond to your stress in unpleasant situations:

- **Fight:** protesting or fighting in response to stress.

- **Freeze:** being unable to move in response to stress.

- **Flop:** a lethargic, dissociative response to stress.

- **Fawn:** trying to please the person causing the stress to survive it.

- **Flight:** the automatic reaction of running away from a threat.

Remember, the body is designed to protect itself—in other words, to protect you—so its reaction to trauma and perceived threats is warranted. Due to the complex nature of trauma, there is no "bad" way to respond to it. Now, let's take a deep dive into the different stress responses so that you can better understand your reactions in moments of distress.

Responses vary between people. The stress response system activates our minds and bodies to carry out innate behaviors. Noticing which responses apply to you during moments of stress can help you change or avoid unhelpful reactions entirely.

Fight

Stressful situations can cause people to respond with action. In fighting, we become activated to face the threat through anger, confrontation, high energy, and rageful behaviors. For example, someone might shout or behave aggressively to neutralize the potential danger.

The physical expressions of your body getting ready to fight in threatening situations can include

- tightened jaw or fists

- clenched teeth

- kicking or punching

- glaring

- raising your voice

- nausea or knots in the stomach

- anger or aggression

When the fight response is stimulated, the brain signals the body to act from the belief that you can overpower the danger.

Freeze

The freeze response is typical for people who experience intense fear during stressful situations. This response is particularly common in people who routinely felt unsafe from a very young age. Since they had a restricted ability to fend for themselves as children, freezing became the most automatic response to trauma for them.

People who freeze in potentially dangerous situations may develop a tendency to dissociate from reality, which increases vulnerability to anxiety or panic disorders (*A Closer Look at Freeze, The Third Stress Response*, n.d.). The physical expressions of the body preparing to freeze can include

- feeling stuck

- coldness or numbness

- physical stiffness or heaviness of limbs

- a lower heart rate

- restricted breathing or holding of the breath

- a sense of dread or foreboding

The feeling of being afraid becomes like an anchor, weighing people down to the same position and limiting their ability to move. The mind might scream, "Run," but the body is too shocked to do anything.

Flop

The flop response happens when someone becomes utterly unresponsive in an attempt to protect themselves from potential danger (Bachert, 2023). The physical expressions of the body flopping include

- appearing disengaged

- expressing no or limited emotion

- skipping school or work and other important commitments

- seeming in an emotional slump

- hopelessness

- loss of consciousness

- apathy

With flopping, the body shuts down to the point where someone becomes mentally, emotionally, and physically unresponsive. Similar to an animal dropping to the floor and playing dead, people in a flop response may faint, curl up, or blackout in response to trauma.

Fawn

People fawn to avoid conflict. It involves doing whatever is asked in an attempt to fulfill the abuser's requests and hopefully minimize the harm. Fawning can make you abandon your needs and values to avoid conflict and criticism from the other person.

People who fawn can

- pursue a career to please parents.

- stay silent about their preferences so that others can have their way.

- self-sabotage for the sake of caring for someone else.

- do things like appeasing or complimenting an abuser at their own expense.

Trauma can make people agreeable in an attempt to "please and appease" to make the experience disappear—that's the root of fawning.

Flight

Sometimes, the body feels the only way to escape or prevent trauma is to run from the threat. While in flight mode, the body experiences a surge of hormones, such as adrenaline and cortisol. These hormones give your body the energy to gear up and flee from danger faster than usual.

The physical expressions of the body preparing to flee include

- avoidance

- panic

- restlessness

- tension

- rapid moving legs, arms, and feet

- a rush of adrenalin

- darting eyes

- stress

- feeling overwhelmed

- anxiety

Our biological instinct is to control situations. So, when we are in positions where that sense of safety and control is removed, our bodies go into response mode: fight, flight, flop, freeze, or fawn. Any one of these responses can occur.

Early development in childhood can massively impact our default responses as adults. Our ability to defend ourselves is limited in the early stages of growth. A lot of the time, our fate is in the hands of our parents and caregivers, so if we feel unsafe during those crucial moments of development, it creates memories of trauma in our bodies. This can lead to freezing, fighting, fleeing, fawning, or flopping in the face of adversity.

Trauma Triggers

The physical and emotional responses to trauma can continue long after the event as a result of exposure to traumatic triggers. This refers to any stimuli—such as events, experiences, or behaviors—that spark symptoms of traumatic stress. Triggers can make us feel past experiences as though they are happening now. People with a history of trauma are highly susceptible to being triggered.

Trauma is complex, and so is how triggers form The following steps explain how triggers arise for some people:

1. Traumatic experience: The first step of how triggers form is the experience of something traumatic. When you are in an unpleasant situation, it causes strong emotional reactions.

2. Association: Once you react strongly, your mind starts associating the experience with your environment. For example, certain sounds, smells, areas, and behaviors can be related to a specific trauma experience. The association typically occurs unconsciously.

3. Memory storage: Now, your mind stores your experience and its associations in your memory. This leaves room for any of the possible stimuli to re-evoke the intense emotions you felt from your trauma experience. The event could have happened years ago, but your brain's association can make it feel like it's happening to you now.

4. Trigger: At this point, every time you encounter a stimulus that pulls from a stored memory of something traumatic, you react or respond as though you were in that traumatic place again. For example, you could flop in a high-intensity situation that reminds you of the trauma-related pressure you experienced as a child. You can experience such triggers even if you don't consciously notice the connection between past and present.

Triggers cause us to feel significant, negative emotions that tend to overwhelm us and make us feel powerless in the moment. For example, someone with a history of substance abuse may experience a trigger—losing a friend, a job, or something else meaningful—which can cause a relapse into their addiction. Triggers are delicate parts of trauma recovery, and understanding how to identify the different types empowers you to cope with them in the future—and hopefully prevent re-traumatization.

Different Types of Triggers

After experiencing a trigger, you can feel heavy emotions and negative feelings such as powerlessness, fear, and self-blame. The intensity of these feelings is harmful to mental health. Triggers can also be challenging to address effectively after the experience. The behaviors that emerge after traumatic experiences range from minimal to severe. For example, a minimal behavior would be crying, while severe behavior examples include aggression or poor choices.

A range of stimuli can create environments of possible triggers. These can be external, internal, trauma, and symptom triggers strongly influenced by past experiences. While triggers are uncomfortable and frustrating, each one is an opportunity to learn how to manage trauma and improve unwanted behaviors or outcomes in the future.

External Triggers

The things that happen outside of yourself are external triggers. Consider different smells, lights, and noises as discussed earlier; these could evoke a memory of something you may have buried deep inside yourself. For example, smelling a particular cologne worn by an abusive ex-lover can trigger fear or hypervigilance.

Internal Triggers

Inversely, internal triggers are the feelings and thoughts that happen within—sometimes due to external factors. For example, going back to a hospital after tragically losing a loved one can stimulate grief, which acts as an internal trigger. Likewise, while failing a test may not be directly linked to any traumatic experience, it could prompt self-berating thoughts that are reminiscent of past emotional abuse and, thus, triggering.

Trauma Triggers

Anything that happens causing you to experience a memory or feeling associated directly with trauma is a trauma trigger. For example, surviving domestic abuse can make you sensitive to aggressive movement, so you might feel triggered when someone raises their voice or slams a surface in frustration.

Symptom Triggers

This refers to triggering symptoms that can happen as a result of trauma. For example, you might struggle to sleep for a while due to ongoing trauma experiences. Sleeplessness can then trigger symptoms of depression.

You might not be able to control your triggers completely, but learning about them can help you prepare better for future responses.

Mental Health Conditions Arising From Trauma

Persistent experiences of trauma can make you vulnerable to mental health issues. However, it's important to understand that mental health issues aren't inevitable outcomes of trauma. People can experience trauma and not develop mental health issues. Examples of mental health conditions include post-traumatic stress disorder (PTSD) and acute stress disorder.

Post-Traumatic Stress Disorder

PTSD is a condition that develops when people are exposed to severe or ongoing trauma. A range of events can cause PTSD, including sexual assault, severe injury, natural disasters, war, neglect, and life-threatening illnesses. People who experience PTSD are known to demonstrate high levels of stress hormones that can cause emotional numbness and hyperarousal over time. Some significant symptoms of PTSD are flashbacks, panic attacks, and thoughts of self-harm.

Acute Stress Disorder

Acute stress disorder tends to begin within the first month after a traumatic experience (Kivi, 2018). People with this disorder can display similar symptoms to those with PTSD. The only distinction is that this disorder lasts a few days to one month after the unpleasant encounter.

Attachment Disorders

These all go back to childhood. Attachment disorders describe conditions that cause difficulties in relating to others. People fortunate enough to grow up in secure environments with responsive caregivers or parents are more likely to develop secure attachments. That allows those people to form genuine, long-lasting connections characterized by trust. On the other hand, people who experience turmoil during those essential years can develop insecure attachments. These are represented by fear and mistrust of people, making it hard to form genuine relationships. Not everyone who has insecure attachments is diagnosed with an attachment disorder, however.

Attachment disorders are marked by a lack of emotional responsiveness or excessive emotional investment in others. A lack of emotional responsiveness can look cold in moments requiring empathy and compassion. Excessive emotional investment, on the other hand, is a borderline obsession with someone else that can create an environment for controlling behaviors to thrive.

Interactive Part 2: How Trauma Affects You

Identifying personal trauma effects, whether conscious or subconscious, is a step toward trauma transformation. Engaging with the following self-reflection questions can help you unpack how trauma affects you.

What are some triggers you have experienced in your life?

_____

_____

_____

Do specific scenarios repeat?

_____

_____

_____

How can you tell when you are triggered?

_____

_____

_____

What common emotions do you feel during a trauma-triggering experience?

_____

_____

_____

Chapter 3:

What the World Doesn't Realize—Can We Address the Experience of Trauma as African American Women?

Devastating events that happen in life can cause adverse physical and emotional outcomes in the form of trauma. Abuse, discrimination, natural disasters, racism, and military combat are examples of experiences of trauma. Enduring years of abuse, abandonment, and other forms of trauma is heavy. Recognizing the root of the difficulties that stem from these sources can help you process personal and generational trauma.

A significant product of colonialism and past racial discrimination is the trauma passed down intergenerationally. For African Americans who were born in enslaved communities, trauma is an ongoing experience, particularly for Black women. The trauma that has been passed down through generations causes issues with self-esteem, internalized oppression, and adverse health outcomes. It's essential to address the experience of African American women to prevent these issues and find healthy ways to deal with modern systems that still oppress Black communities.

The social, economic, and health disparities between Black and White Americans are perpetuated through structural racism (Gillespie, 2023). In this chapter, the trauma of African American people is explored to give insight into the experiences that Black women face today. Conveying this history while unpacking modern-day experiences lays the foundation for the healing Black women so deeply deserve.

The Dawn of Racism and Injustice in the United States

Racism and inequality encompass a systematic separation and mistreatment of African Americans in the US. Injustice and racial inequality toward Black communities have been documented since the 1600s, even though systematic oppression extends across millennia (Miller, 2023). The dawn of racism and injustice in the US was acknowledged through enslavement. The colonial era saw Africans experience dehumanization and demoralization at the hands of White supremacists (believers in complete White control). Many Africans were stripped of their dignity and right to humanity, acceptance, and belonging.

As I'm sure you are aware, our African ancestors were traded as slaves from country to country and used for military conquest. There is collective Black trauma in the fact that our ancestors were seen as objects to be commoditized rather than people who deserved rights and respect. European ships brought with them millions of Black people to multiple plantations in the Americas (Miller, 2023). It's here that Africans were enslaved and forced to provide free labor. By the late 1800s, the domestic slave trade was a major enterprise in the US. Between the 1830s and 1850s, more than 193,000 enslaved Africans were brought across state lines. Since then, and after the 1863 emancipation proclamation, white people have enjoyed the benefits of this oppressive system.

Though enslaved Africans are said to have been emancipated in the late 1800s, many didn't understand or weren't informed of this "freedom." Therefore, many enslaved people continued to live impoverished lives marked by physical illness, starvation, and chronic trauma. To prove that racism and slavery were still persistent in many parts of America, the Jim Crow laws (reinforcing racial segregation) were beginning to be instated as early as 1896 and were not theoretically abolished until 1965. Practically, however, racism continued to run rampant. Segregation laws created massive confusion and misinformation, perpetuating the idea that African Americans should be grateful for being "equal" to their white counterparts but remain separate from them. In honor of these segregation laws, African Americans were provided "the same"—but separate and lower-standard—facilities as white people.

Racial segregation continued the principles of slavery by institutionalizing politics, culture, education, and many other systems to ensure that Black people remained at an inferior level (systematically) to white people. Once Black people were indeed "free" to begin living on their personal terms, it was already built off the back of a history of trauma.

Generational Trauma in African American Women

Research done in the 1940s showed how trauma passed down generationally negatively influences the self-image of young Black children (Asare, 2022). So, generational trauma starts impacting Black women from a young age. The research from the '40s showed that when young Black kids were asked to choose between a Black and a White doll, their preference was the latter. It was evident that, from a young age, Black children are influenced by their and their ancestors' traumatic pasts.

Throughout history, Black women might have internalized traumas from their ancestors. Many Black youth learn helplessness through intergenerational oppression, especially people from under-resourced communities. The feeling and experience of being trapped in situations you can't change as a child translates into frustration as an adult. Experiencing firsthand or secondary trauma contributes to feelings of helplessness. The trap of enslavement didn't just come to an end when the Emancipation Proclamation came into play. There are still ways that that past trauma manifests in the modern day

We live in societies and economies where African American people are kept in invisible chains. Not to mention how the African American woman is at the very bottom of the social priority list. To quote Malcolm X, "The most disrespected person in America is the Black woman. The most unprotected person in America is the Black woman. The most neglected person in America is the Black woman (*Malcolm X: 'The Most Disrespected Person in America, is The Black Woman,' Speech to Women–1964*, n.d.).

Fast forward from slavery, and African Americans continue to live under oppression in a society that refuses to see us for our excellence. From our Black brothers and sisters being killed by those who are sworn to "protect and serve" to having to work four times harder for less pay Things may have changed in theory, but racism and trauma still prevail.

Present-Day Experiences of Trauma

Generational trauma leaves lasting scars on overall well-being. It impacts entire family structures as well as self-belief. Some manifestations of generational trauma affecting present-day experiences include distance within families, neglect (of self and others), trauma bonding, and self-esteem issues. Anxiety, depression, and PTSD are all effects that can come from generational trauma. Due to the burden of past experiences, it's common for Black women to find it hard to escape the cycle of trauma. However, it being hard doesn't mean it's impossible.

Young African American women are highly vulnerable to racial trauma, especially if they have not processed the weight of the past fully yet (Miller, 2023). Women are continually affected by the consequences of racial segregation, injustice, and racism. Present-day trauma has compounded pain from past dealings, whether modern or from the past. The trauma African Americans experienced centuries ago still bleeds into the present. Modern-day racism is marked by other forms of oppression and discrimination, mainly manifesting as microaggressive behaviors.

Microaggressions are statements, behaviors, and actions that are prejudiced or discriminatory toward marginalized communities. Whether intentional or unintentional, microaggressions are hurtful, and you are valid in feeling upset when you are in the crossfire. It can be beneficial to know the three multiple types of microaggressions: microinsults, microinvalidations, and microassaults. Breaking down behaviors and noticing the signs of these aggressions will validate your reality in situations where people try to undermine your pain.

Microinsults

Microinsults are subtle conversations, behaviors, and hidden communications that demean someone's racial background. Insults like this can be overtly disrespectful, for example, "She's an angry person," referring to a black colleague. However, they can also be subtle and disguised as compliments. If someone says, "Wow, you speak so eloquently (compared to people of your kind)," it's an example of a microinsult. These comments are typically rude and insensitive and leave you feeling down about yourself.

Consider a scenario where you are conversing with a barista at a coffee shop. With a blank, surprised stare, she turns to you and says, "Your English is remarkable. Are you from here?" This implies that your English is too broad for someone "like you." In other words, she believes that Black people don't speak or sound as educated as you.

Microinvalidations

Microinvalidations are expressions that deny, exclude, devalue, and dismiss someone's thoughts, feelings, beliefs, and contributions based on their racial background. These are common in society, especially when people are afraid of appearing racist or villainous. For example, being told that a topic has nothing to do with race, even though it does. I'm sure you know people who do or say things that are racially motivated or ignorant, then proceed to deny them with one comment: "This isn't about race," or "I have Black friends; I'd never do that."

Black women are regularly invalidated in this way, especially in hospitals. For example, a woman who needs medical care for frequent pains is likely to bump into a doctor who barely hears her concerns but prescribes anxiety medication and encourages a follow-up appointment weeks down the line. Yet, the same doctor is more attentive and patient with another woman who walks in with the same issue, prescribing pain relief and scans to check for underlying issues. I bet you can guess which woman is Black—the first.

Microassaults

Unlike other microaggressions, microassaults are more deliberate because they intend to harm marginalized people (Lockett, 2023). Microassaults are explicit practices intended to harm someone of color, and these can include name-calling, avoidance, and discrimination. Some examples of microassaults are "those people," "your group," or "people like you." Microassaults are usually explicit forms of prejudice that vary between subtle and obviously apparent.

Imagine a scenario where you are waiting at your terminal at the airport; you choose to sit next to someone. This person had been sitting in the same seat minutes before you came. Suddenly, the person gets up and finds another seat to avoid sitting next to you; that is a microassault. Discrimination is at play when someone who knows nothing about you blatantly seems nervous or uncomfortable beside you. These things, unfortunately, happen far too often.

The African American women's experience of the world is a culmination of our traumatic history and modern-day microaggressions. We live in a world with people who tolerate us simply because the law tells them to. Someone who hasn't spent a day in the shoes of a Black woman has no idea of the burdens we carry daily. Between fighting the world and masking as "strong" to survive it, all our magic can be lost in there. It's essential to use this knowledge and rise about these oppressions. Pouring into ourselves is how we overcome the subtle discriminations of the world. We might not be able to change how others view and treat us, but we can transform how we treat ourselves. It changes our perception of how we need to carry ourselves.

We need not apologize for our existence nor pretend that these issues aren't part of our reality. Instead, we must be bold in accepting ourselves and everything that comes with being Black women. This acceptance leads to self-love—a love so strong that it can address iniquities in self-compassionate ways without being consumed by them or disempowered in the process. Sure, our trauma is a part of the story, but it isn't the end. The next chapter explores the "strong Black woman" narrative and unpacks how this can rob us of our rightful humanity.

Chapter 4:

Trauma and Its Branches—

How the "Strong Black

Woman" Narrative Affects Us

Traditionally, African American women managed trauma and stress by repeating the "strong Black woman" narrative. For years, this has been known to empower Black women with the resilience needed to make it in the world. We've been taught to swallow our feelings, repress our stories, and mute our voices. Though Black women are strong, this narrative's hidden meaning is that we are something beyond human. We are expected to cope with pain more internally than most people and with a smile on our faces or risk being slapped with an even more cutting trope: the *angry* Black woman. Because of this narrative, in America, Black women are less likely to seek help compared to their racial counterparts.

From an early age, Black girls are socialized to internalize the idea of projected strength out of the belief that it serves as armor and resilience. Little girls have grown up watching their mothers wear this mask in an attempt to resist oppression and overcome challenges in America. Yet, research demonstrates that this socialization has more psychological detriments than it does benefits (Jones et al., 2020). Internalizing concepts such as independence, emotional restraint, and personal sacrifice—

which are ideals associated with the strong Black woman narrative—are linked to a multitude of adverse mental health outcomes.

The emotional pain of Black women has been sidelined for ages. Yet, African American women experience more stress at work, with finances, and as a result of home responsibilities because of the additional weight of sexism, racism, and trauma (Burnett-Zeigler, 2022). Issues such as the COVID-19 pandemic and police brutality toward members of the Black community exacerbate this stress and contribute to mental health difficulties. Yet, despite this, we are expected to be "strong."

However, growing research around this topic is starting to expose the consequences of the narrative. These discoveries and lived experiences push young Black women to interrogate the concept of being strong and hopefully redefine the meaning of strength for themselves. This chapter explores the "strong Black woman" narrative and its effects on young women in particular. It also analyzes the three aspects that drive this stereotype and its influence on mental health.

Staying Strong When We Want to Be Soft: What It Means to Be "Strong Black Women"

Generations of Black mothers almost single-handedly raised children, nurtured the bonds of strong families, and skillfully pulled limited resources together to ensure everyone's needs were met. To top it all off, Black women did it all with love. Even historically, Black women made personal sacrifices to ensure the happiness and freedom of future generations. Rosa Parks, Ruby Hurley, and Dorothy Heights are examples of such courageous women who fought, spoke up, marched, and challenged the status quo in the past. Lineages of women—many of them mothers and grandmothers—led revolutions while navigating the worst of institutionalized gender and racial oppression; that's where the stereotype came from.

The strong Black woman narrative has been a source of pride for many. The idea began to empower Black women during dire moments when life seemed to be breaking us down. However, this narrative became tainted over time. When the label went from celebrating the strengths of Black women to expecting that we never show our vulnerabilities, it became a health hazard. The tough side of being strong as a Black woman is that the world begins to have all these unrealistic standards for us. Needing to constantly be strong is burdensome for anyone, but it is especially draining for Black women in a world so polarizing that we are still celebrating Black people for being "the first" or "the only" in particular spaces. Things like this continue to trigger traumas associated with segregation.

Being "the first" Black woman CEO of a massive corporate company, for example, is a reminder of marginalization. It almost puts a stamp on the sense that we don't belong. This increases the pressure to aspire to be perfect and the demand to be twice as resilient. After all, "the strong Black woman" can't have her own fears. Even if she does, she's expected to hide them or "suck it up." The narrative of the strong Black woman intensifies self-monitoring because it seems like everywhere we go, we are carrying the burden on our backs. If we make a mistake, we quickly go from the most "impressive" in the company to inadvertently proving stereotypes about Black women.

We are expected to display a level of resilience that hides vulnerability, and most of our humanity becomes embedded in our trauma and suffering. This leads to personal battles of depression and anxiety that perpetuate the cycle of breaking us down. Staying strong when we want to be soft keeps us silent when overwhelmed. This silence worsens our experience of isolation and heaviness. Yet, by putting that cloak of strength down, we can indeed exist in our power.

Giving voice to our experiences and trauma empowers us to break free from the strong Black woman narrative. It provides us the keys to unlock the cage of superficial strength and embrace that some parts of us must be held too. If we want to stay healthy, we must accept that we cannot always be strong, and we shouldn't have to pretend to be either.

Instead, we can embrace our humanity just as much as everyone else. It's helpful to affirm that it's okay for us to balance being strong and soft. Holding space for our stories, trauma, and pain is good. Equally, celebrating that we are more than those things is even better. Giving ourselves space to find balance allows us to embrace our identity holistically with compassion and grace, understanding that we are worthy as we are. Collectively, we are far more capable than we think. And as an individual, you have it in you to be both strong and vulnerable. A combination of these things empowers you to live in your truth. Balancing your softness and strength reminds you that you can be more than any stereotype. After all, you are more than your trauma.

The Mental and Emotional Toll of This Stereotype

Though it was intended as a celebratory statement, the stereotype is also very harmful because being a "strong Black woman" can take a significant toll on overall health. This stereotype paints Black women as lacking in uniqueness or being unfeeling, angry, aggressive, and indifferent toward people. What's more, our character comes into question when we can no longer accept the mistreatment and manipulation connected to this stereotype.

The women who came before us carried the world's burdens and managed to portray strong, composed personas, never showing any vulnerability. Now, the expectation is for us to follow that example across all aspects of our lives—at work, in relationships, in our homes, and within our communities—often at the expense of our well-being and energy. The expectation is that since we are "strong Black women," we should be able to take poor treatment and handle adversity gracefully. So, when colleagues, friends, and other people in social spaces mistreat us, we are expected to roll with the punches as the strong Black women we are. Doing so takes a huge toll on our mental health.

Research by Castelin et al. (2022) found that the strong Black woman narrative has negative implications for psychological well-being. Black women who suppress emotions (a symptom of trauma) to uphold the narrative are seen to have higher reports of distress (the trauma itself) and suicidal behaviors. Suicide is one of the primary causes of death in America, and it is an undeniable result of suicidal behaviors. Examples of such behaviors are suicidal ideation (constantly having thoughts of self-harm), threats of taking one's life, and attempts to commit the act. Additionally, Black women who uphold this narrative have a higher risk of developing PTSD compared to their White counterparts. Carrying suffering for the sake of survival has been a badge of honor for generations of Black women, and this stereotype triggers that trauma. Castelin et al. (2022) also highlight that Black women who uphold the narrative of being strong are twice as likely to receive a diagnosis of major depressive disorder.

Striving to uphold this narrative is so harmful that women in sports chose to launch a movement for the sake of the mental well-being of Black women. For example, tennis multi-champion Naomi Osaka and Olympic gymnast Simone Biles decided not to compete at specific points in their lives to protect their mental health. This shows that the stereotype of being a strong Black woman shouldn't be exclusionary; we should be able to talk about our tough days without feeling ashamed or "weak" for it. Vulnerability is essential; if anything, it is a form of strength in itself. Black women are the bedrock of society, and we matter, so our mental health is essential and should be prioritized.

When the Young Black Girl Becomes a Strong Black Woman

The strong Black woman narrative can be damaging for young black girls if they only pick up on the negative cues as opposed to the balanced, more celebrated concept that it was meant to be. Mothers stay in abusive situations or hide their tears as examples of this unrealistic resilience that Black women are supposed to convey. Studies show that little Black girls are often viewed through this stereotype as well (Fleming, n.d.-a). Even in a group of young peers, Black girls are seen as stronger, more mature, and knowledgeable about the world. This stereotype plays out in the lack of support that Black girls receive in school compared to their White friends. It is the reason why, many times, young Black girls who misbehave in class are treated much differently—or worse—than young White girls with the same behaviors.

Also, the probability is higher of a young Black girl being punished for misbehaving at school compared to her White friends. Research confirms that Black girls are at least 10 times more likely to be punished with suspension from school and related activities compared to girls of other races (Fleming, n.d.-a). This is how the strong Black woman narrative plays out for little Black girls who need gentle guidance as much as every other kid.

It doesn't stop there; the mistreatment of Black girls is perpetuated in society. Research shows that police are more likely to use excessive force against Black girls, especially teenagers, compared to their White peers (Fleming, n.d.-a). Though the findings don't directly connect the harsh treatment of Black girls to the stereotype, it's clear that this preconceived idea of Black strength influences reality.

Black girls grow up feeling like the only way to survive the world is to be strong, unbothered, and determined. It's easy to identify with struggle and see hard armor as necessary. Information from this stereotype and how the world treats Black girls can make you absorb the idea that asking for help is a weakness. You can grow up believing you are on your own—that if you don't help yourself, no one else will. Black girls become strong Black women because it's what they see growing up. Every example at home, school, and other social circles repeats this narrative. We are taught early that speaking up makes us "angry Black women," and staying silent about our needs *is* true strength.

It's challenging and confusing to go into the world and be told to act in one way or another. Upholding the strong Black woman narrative is mentally exhausting and does no favors for the person wearing the title. It is hard enough to be strong for your family as they navigate generational trauma and for yourself as you manage societal pressures without feeling the weight of being strong for the rest of the world too.

The Three Underlying Factors That Drive the Stereotype

To uphold the strong Black woman narrative, the prerequisite is to overcome adversity through unparalleled strength and personal sacrifice. This is a condition that has roots in colonialism and slavery, spurred on by the intergenerational trauma of women of African descent—Black women. The idea of strong Black women is built on three underlying factors: the mask of resilience, self-reliance, and caregiving (White 2017).

These factors temporarily help us to overcome discrimination, but they are not sustainable solutions, especially for women who want to live boldly, lively, and happily.

The Mask of Resilience

Emotional invulnerability is at the core of masking with resilience. The idea that Black women should hide their struggles or pretend to be carrying them better than everyone else is the mask we've learned to put on. There are many drawbacks to believing that we must be "superwomen" to cope with challenges such as racial discrimination and sexism. For instance, this causes us to wear emotional armor and feel obligated to present an image of resilience even when we might not feel very strong. The mask of resilience causes us to suppress and disregard our emotions in an attempt to survive them. We end up not speaking up about how we feel, which is detrimental to our health.

Self-Reliance

The strong Black woman is expected to be independent beyond the natural meaning of the word. Our self-reliance says, "I don't need anyone because I can do it on my own." Yet, everyone needs community to thrive and be healthy. Along with the mask of resilience, we are socialized to be okay with doing things on our own and to believe that doing so is commendable. So, we practice self-reliance and build walls that keep us from genuinely connecting to others. This self-isolation can sometimes add a layer to the trauma, resulting in depression and anxiety symptoms along with others.

Caregiving

This strong Black woman narrative factor refers to the long-existing drive that we have to help others, sometimes at our own expense. Black women carry so much pressure, internally and externally. The world expects one thing of us, and we work overtime to fulfill personal standards for how we want to be. The emphasis put on caregiving makes us prioritize everyone else before ourselves. Therefore, Black women are less likely to ask for help when needed (White, 2021).

Since socialization starts in childhood, we pick up the standards of resilience, self-reliance, and caregiving very early. Not only does this take an emotional toll on each person who internalizes these values, but it also continues to hurt their inner child. Even as adults, there are children in each of us (our inner child) who need care, reparenting, and unlearning to heal from the traumas we are subjected to. In the next chapter, we explore this concept of the inner child to find out what it is and how to heal it.

Chapter 5:

The Inner Child and Trauma

Everyone has an inner child. This refers to a younger version of oneself that holds every experience. The inner child is a significant part of the subconscious that influences an adult's thoughts and reactions. It's most often used in therapy and spiritual settings as a symbol of the difficulties, victories, and trauma that we went through during childhood.

Your inner child has been part of you since birth and through your developmental years. It's the part of you that grows with you from the baby stage and middle school all the way to adulthood. Early childhood and the younger years of your life influence your inner child's habits and responses. Good experiences lead to healthier responses and memories, while the opposite is true for tough experiences.

It's important to understand the inner child to grow self-awareness. Ignoring the inner child is subsequently ignoring the influences of the past on your beliefs, thoughts, and emotions in the present. You can end up doing yourself a disservice and overlooking some significant formative encounters that are crucial to trauma recovery and healing. Being willing to understand your inner child allows you to overcome certain ideals that trauma has created. It also helps you change unhelpful behaviors and learn more effective coping mechanisms.

Trauma often starts during childhood, so understanding what your inner child has endured is the beginning of personal healing. This chapter explores what the inner child is, why it's essential, and how you can start reconnecting with yours.

Understanding Your Inner Child: The Trauma and Strength Within

Your inner child is the part of yourself that holds childhood memories, feelings, and beliefs. Carl Jung, a psychiatrist and psychoanalyst interested in understanding human behavior, initially highlighted the inner child concept (Heyl, 2023). Your inner child can motivate your daily choices and feelings without you being aware of them.

Think of the inner child as the young person you were during your most pivotal period. You might feel disconnected from your younger self as you age, but starting the reconnection process is beneficial. When you aren't knowledgeable of your inner child, you lose awareness of a distinct part of yourself. This lack of awareness can make life as an adult hard because you could find yourself dealing with things from a regressive perspective during moments of frustration. For example, you might respond to something frustrating with aggression due to lower emotional regulation. Lower regulation can be highly attributed to trauma as a child when you felt unheard or dismissed by your parents. However, the inability to link those emotions to your childhood makes it challenging to deal with present-day experiences.

Another example is battling to cope with feelings of loneliness and shame and instead having an angry outburst—similar to a tantrum. Yet, once you start noticing the patterns in your responses, you soon realize they are your inner child communicating. Your inner child often recalls your childhood experiences: The good things that happened during childhood are stored in your mind, but the inner child also remembers the bad. Your fears, traumas, and significant losses are stored in your subconscious too. These guide how you see the world and your beliefs about what and who you can and can't trust.

Understanding your inner child by listening and starting an internal dialogue can help you shift your traumas into positive ammunition.

Signs of a wounded inner child

- frustration or irritation

- strong reactions to unmet needs

- childish outbursts (like throwing tantrums or saying things you don't mean)

- complaining that no one understands you or you don't feel heard

- difficulty explaining your feelings or why you're upset (alexithymia)

- low self-esteem

- harsh inner critic

- patterns of self-sabotage

- fear of abandonment or commitment issues

- challenges with setting boundaries or expressing your needs

Your wounded inner child will appear in your daily experiences. You might find yourself being super reactive in triggering situations. Suddenly, you notice yourself being detached and frustrated right after something unpleasant happens due to your internal discomfort. Your adult self is so attached to your younger self that one cannot experience life without influencing the other. You might even find that you repeat the strong Black woman narrative by overvaluing independence. Sure, striving for an independent life where you can provide for yourself and take care of your needs is great. However, an overly independent life overvalues being alone. It can even lead you to sever important connections for the sake of self-reliance. If you find yourself constantly repeating, "I don't need anyone," or " I can do it on my own," then you might be living in a past childhood wound.

The inability to ask for help but instead take up resilience and nonemotionality is also a sign of the wounded inner child. You are like everyone else; therefore, you should feel safe enough to ask for assistance when needed. Not being able to do so shows that your inner child needs you to reparent them in a way that allows comfort around the topic.

A wounded inner child can even have destructive coping mechanisms. You might not always deal with things in beneficial ways, which can show in your adult choices. For example, overconsumption of alcohol, gambling, cheating, and binging on or harshly restricting food are signs of destructive coping. These can result from your inner child needing something. Maybe, they need you to trust yourself, so they can stop gravitating toward these vices.

When your inner child is triggered, certain wounds resurface that can cause you to be a volatile adult or overcompensate in situations where you should be comfortable asking for help. Inner child triggers can happen in daily life over what might seem like the most straightforward situations. For example, if you were always judged for your mistakes as a child, you could develop a hyperawareness of the things you don't do right. As a result, arriving late for a meeting could trigger feelings of incompetence, self-condemnation, and fear—all of which align with how you felt when you made mistakes as a child. Rather than knowing that it's okay to be flawed, your inner child might feel like being late for the meeting is the end of the world, particularly if your caregivers made you feel that way growing up.

Experiences of instability, shame, yelling, and abuse as a child tend to influence self-perception as an adult. Of course, your inner child isn't just a trauma carrier. The inner child is also present in your core when you are happy or laughing. That's why it's sometimes easier to find excuses for poor parental behaviors than it is to hold our parents accountable for some of the things they did to contribute to our trauma. For example, someone with an absent mother might argue that the neglect was justified because "Mom had to work." Though the inner child is still left confused and upset by their upbringing, the adult remembers how mom would take the younger self to parks on her off days, which showed them love. The subconscious remembers the good and the bad, which is why trauma can be so complex. Your upbringing could hurt you but also give you some memories to cherish.

Think back to a moment when you were delighted; that giddy part of yourself represents moments of enjoyment for your inner child. It exemplifies a positive inner child trigger that saw you feel hopeful, even in dire situations. Trauma doesn't override the good that happened as a child. If anything, the mind might even favor the good memories and suppress the bad. Suppression makes it hard to understand some of your inner child triggers. Yet, it would help if you found ways to work through them. Whatever is suppressed doesn't stay down for long; emotional suppression expresses itself through behaviors and responses, and that's why it's important to unpack childhood experiences so that you can increase awareness.

All of this is especially true for a Black child. We grow up being taught that suffering is inherited through our bloodlines. While some people have a generational inpouring of privilege and stability, African American children already deal with a chip on their shoulders. Where you come from a violent background, have an absent parent or parents, were raised in poverty, or had fewer resources than your peers growing up, there is a scar that you carry. We carry this into a world that has preset assumptions about how we stereotypically act and how we should be.

Your inner child recalls the fun from your upbringing together with your trauma. It isn't easy to pinpoint the particular moment or experience that impacts your feelings and reactions. Still, you can start to understand these as communications from your inner child so that you can begin the reparenting process.

The Process of Reparenting Your Inner Child

Reparenting your inner child is a process that acknowledges childhood trauma and works to heal what comes up. It's an approach to adulting that recognizes that your behaviors in adulthood come from your experiences as a child. Giving your inner child a voice is an approach that focuses on identifying your unmet needs and being attentive to them. Reparenting helps you understand your behaviors, triggers, desires, and needs.

The benefits of reparenting include

- self-awareness and understanding of personal trauma.

- develop healthy coping skills.

- self-control and feeling empowered.

- improved self-regulation.

- higher self-esteem, self-compassion, and empathy for others.

Starting a healthy dialogue with your inner child is how you begin reparenting yourself. This process aims to allow your inner child to feel care, validation, love, and nurture—all the things you may have lacked sufficient amounts of during your upbringing. You can nurture the little kid in you and validate the emotions that came from having unmet needs. This is an opportunity to reassure your younger self that you are emotionally safe, even after an unsafe childhood and in an unsafe world. Reparenting allows you to be your own sense of comfort, so you can heal the child and become a better, more confident adult. The process of parenting helps build trust with yourself too. You get to let your inner child experience how it feels to have the attention and love of a competent adult. This is about protecting your younger self at all costs.

By reparenting your inner child, you create an environment for healing. This helps with self-improvement and living beyond trauma. Reparenting is a step toward mental clarity, emotional health, and self-awareness. Your inner child constantly communicates with you; listening to these guides is how you start reparenting yourself.

How to Reparent

Your inner child is either calm and content, irritable and rumbly, or a mixture of all those things at different times. The mannerisms that your inner child displays can hinder your relationships, management skills, and self-regulation. Learning to listen to your inner child's needs can help you develop a healthy life that defies your trauma.

Emotions are signals of what your inner child needs from moment to moment. For example, frustration can indicate that your inner child needs attention. Feeling frustrated or stuck at specific points in your life is your inner child saying, "Hey, this is overwhelming, and I just need you to talk to me right now." Observing your inner child and attending to them is beneficial. So, when you feel frustrated, you can place one of your hands on your chest, close your eyes to imagine your younger self, and then breathe in, saying, "I'm safe and progressing," before exhaling.

Sometimes, you may notice yourself feeling afraid, anxious, or perfectionistic; your inner child might even communicate through avoidance. You could notice yourself avoiding certain situations, environments, and people who trigger unpleasant emotions. In many ways, this is how your inner child expresses fear, discomfort, or feeling unsafe.

When your inner child controls your responses, you'll notice yourself experiencing behaviors or making decisions based on subconscious beliefs. You may even question why you said certain things or how you responded after the fact. The inner child isn't aware of the adult experiences of reality, so they can't understand how things are different now unless you teach them over time. Your inner child still lives as the younger version of yourself, and it needs you to help it grow.

Your adult self feels what your inner child feels, so caring for yourself in tough times helps to overcome strong emotions. During reparenting, allowing your inner child to feel emotionally validated, accepted, cared for, and forgiven is crucial. You can reconnect with your inner child by setting boundaries, doing self-care daily, and embracing every ounce of who you are.

Emotional Validation and Regulation

When you feel upset or emotional about something, it's your inner child trying to tell you something. Pay attention to what's happening around you, who you're talking to, and your environment. It's essential to understand what triggers point to childhood wounds. Emotional wounds heal when you listen to your inner child and let them know you are there for them.

Feeling like your needs were unmet as a child can lead to unhelpful patterns that can only be broken by validating and loving yourself. To practice emotional self-validation, you can start journaling your feelings daily and speaking to yourself like you would to a child you care about. Say something like, "It's okay that I feel this way because I was hurt by [name the person or people] in this way." Start pointing out your experiences and reassuring your inner child that your emotions are valid. This reassurance is the first step to changing how you process and respond when those emotions are triggered. For example, you can learn to walk away and take deep breaths when you feel triggered rather than have a meltdown or throw a tantrum.

Besides journaling, do your best to remember what your inner child needs throughout the day. Mindfulness involves practicing empathy on days when you don't feel your best and observing your emotions without judgment. Learn to name what you are feeling ("I feel angry"), and don't condemn yourself; instead, let the feeling be. Emotional validation is all about meeting yourself where you are.

Setting Boundaries

Unprocessed trauma might appear in a lack of boundaries or a range thereof. When you start to set boundaries, you permit yourself to be free from needing external validation. Boundaries help you say "no" to other people without feeling shame. You can start with small boundaries. For example, if your coworker expects you to take on some of their work but you are overwhelmed with your own, saying "no" is important. Boundaries help you maintain energy and prevent manipulation from others. You can draw the line about what you are and aren't willing to do.

Accepting Your Imperfections

Everyone has flaws, and it's vital to notice and embrace your own. Imperfections make you human. They don't mean you "deserve" what you've been through. Accepting your imperfections humanizes you to yourself so that you can treat yourself gently. In turn, this helps you accept other people's flaws, too.

Self-Forgiveness

Sometimes, trauma can make you take on shame that doesn't even belong to you. Self-forgiveness is about letting go of all the weight you've carried through resentment toward yourself. Maybe, you are upset about how long it has taken for you to acknowledge generational trauma and finally work to heal your inner child. However, this is the opportunity to forgive yourself for it all. What matters is that you are here and worthy of the goodness that this moment offers you. To practice self-forgiveness, turn to a mirror and say, "I forgive myself for [mention the many things]." Forgiving yourself is important, and it's a restorative process.

You can't change the past, but you can weaken its power over you by committing to the reparenting process. Understanding and caring for your inner child is critical because you are calmer when they are cared for. A more relaxed person is empowered to try new things and embrace change. When your inner child is regulated, you open up to the world and what it offers. You are also better suited to tolerate hardships and mistakes to learn from them. A healed inner child allows you to cope with problems and manage emotions healthily. You become less impulsive and develop more self-control and discipline to accomplish tasks. Reparenting your inner child fosters more stability in your life and increases your confidence in your capabilities. This way, you are less prone to seeking validation from others because you already give that to yourself.

Your inner child feeling safe allows you to be an adult who thrives beyond trauma. Healing and addressing your inner child's wounds will take time, so be patient with yourself. The rewards of going steady and shifting your internal atmosphere are worth being patient. The next chapter explores the concept of inner child healing further to provide you with tools to succeed and be more than your trauma.

Chapter 6:

Healing the Inner Child—a Step Toward Trauma Transformation

Now that you know what your inner child is and how childhood experiences can wound it, it's time to work on the healing. Paying attention to the quiet voice within and looking out for cues from your younger self is important. No matter how old you get, your inner child will be with you daily. Maybe, your wounded seven-year-old self appears when your adult self feels marginalized in spaces such as work or home. Perhaps, you have days when you feel alone and misunderstood, and your inner child needs you to be there for them. Caring for your younger self is how you step toward transforming personal trauma.

Healing the inner child involves creating a mental space where the subconscious can lead. It's going deeper within yourself to explore your emotions and the parts that might have experienced adversity during your upbringing. Some of these parts could have been labeled "inappropriate," "not enough," or "too much" by other people. Thus, your inner child knows no better than to view themselves through that lens. A wounded inner child unconsciously repeats unhelpful patterns of behavior that can negatively impact your productivity and relationships.

By allowing yourself to take the time you need to search inwardly and begin to peel back particular trauma-related layers, you are empowered to live a whole, mindful life of acceptance. You start by integrating your past and present and finding healthy coping methods. Healing your inner child pulls you away from trauma so that you can feel less avoidant, numb, and overwhelmed. It draws you closer to mental clarity, consciousness, and self-acceptance—all of which you need to live an authentic life as a Black woman.

The process of healing your inner child ensures that you are freed from the demands of the "strong Black woman" narrative and can live your most vulnerable and resilient life. Inner child healing addresses your needs—especially those that haven't been met—and heals those wounds to enhance your developmental process. So, if you feel reactive, overly self-reliant, self-destructive, or lacking emotional regulation, these are all signs that your inner child might need healing. This chapter builds on the parenting process mentioned in the previous chapter to help you take the necessary steps toward trauma transformation.

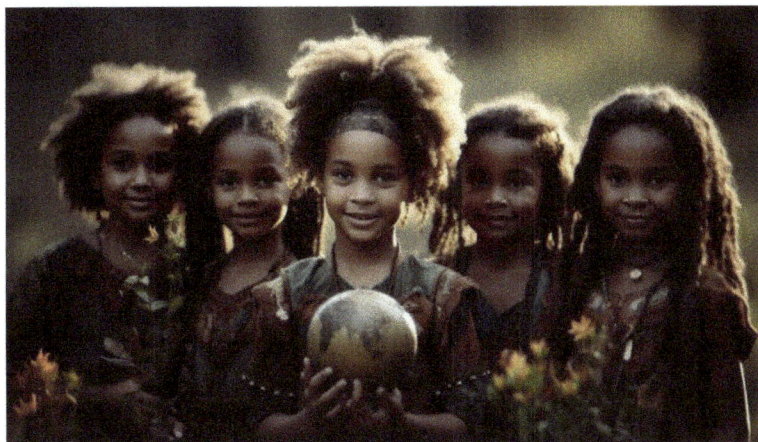

Inner Work to Heal Your Inner Child

Inner child work is an approach toward healing that considers the language and level of understanding of what your younger self needs to thrive. Healing in the field of inner child work focuses on emotional restoration. Examples of trauma therapy that inform inner child work are eye movement desensitization and reprocessing (EMDR), internal family systems, psychotherapy, art therapy, and narrative therapy—approaches that are all rooted in the intention to ignite a healthy connection with your younger self.

As children, we are highly impressionable and affected by how people treat us. We readily absorb behaviors from parents, caregivers, and the environments that we are in while growing up. We internalize these as appropriate patterns to carry through our lives. For example, seeing my mom and dad fight most nights left a massive scar on me. My inner child still grapples with the screams I'd hear at night. Until now, I have been wrestling with the memory of packing our bags in the middle of the night to escape my father's intoxicated, aggressive nature. It's all imprinted within me; my inner child learns to cope with those memories daily.

Without addressing inner child wounds, they grow deeper and become wildly more challenging to heal over time. Wounds are triggered each time someone does something that reminds us of them. For example, a friend publicly humiliating or ignoring you (even unintentionally) could be a huge sore point for an inner child who's struggling with abandonment issues. How you internalize your experiences determines whether or not a wound heals into a scar or stays open.

Like everyone, you are offered a chance to process your wounds and heal them as an adult. As a grown-up, you can heal your inner child's wounds and create a nurturing environment for yourself so that you always feel safe and taken care of.

Healing your inner child is important because you untie the shame that comes with past experiences. You can show yourself more compassion and grace in this life. Whether you have experienced trauma from physical abuse or emotional experiences, you are not alone. There are multiple ways for you to create a safe space for your inner child and unlock positive traits in the process. Navigating inner child healing increases your capacity to love, be adventurous, and accept mistakes. Below are pointers for how you can access and heal your younger self.

Acknowledge Your Inner Child's Experiences

Hurtful early childhood experiences are hard to shake as an adult. However, acknowledging these experiences helps you get emotionally unstuck. Hear yourself out, and be open to the part of yourself that remembers the difficulties you've gone through growing up. Look at yourself in the mirror, and affirm that your experiences are valid and that no one else needs to validate them. Visualize some of the less pleasant experiences you've experienced and ask yourself

- "What did I feel during those moments?"

- "What are some things I regret?"

- "What makes me happy about my childhood?"

- "What saddens me?"

- "How can I heal from these experiences?"

Bringing these memories and hurts into the open can help you start to understand your experience. Shedding light onto your experiences is helpful and often soothing over time. This process allows you to validate your trauma, so you can overcome it. Of course, overcoming trauma isn't something quick or a one-time occurrence. You need to commit, practice, and reinforce positive behaviors to help you daily. It may be uncomfortable, even painful, but nobody knows you better than you do. The more you connect with your inner child, the more you learn about things or feelings you may have forgotten.

Remind your inner child that you are the adult in charge now and that you will ensure they receive the best of everything. Your younger self needs to feel that they have your support regardless of what happens externally. The process of acknowledging your younger self involves bringing awareness and acceptance to the things that caused you pain as a child.

Notice the Parts of Yourself That Are Your Inner Child's Way of Protecting You

When you go through things at a young age, your inner child develops habits to try and protect you from experiencing those same difficulties in the future. Defenses such as avoidance or lashing out from frustration are your inner child's way of standing up for themselves in ways they perhaps couldn't before. However, these defenses can get in the way of healthy habits. Being defensive has a way of separating you from the things that you need to heal. For example, you may pull away from genuine relationships out of fear that you could get hurt.

Consider What You Value About Yourself

The world is used to undervaluing Black women, and it's up to you to pour value back into yourself. Consider what you enjoy about the person you are. Knowing your value is a foundational part of self-awareness. It helps you combat negative perspectives and voices from the external environment. A better understanding of what makes you an asset enables you to develop better regulation and communication skills (Perry, 2023). Being clear about what you value about yourself helps you make purpose-driven choices and decisions. Values shape how you think, feel, contribute to the world, and behave. Some examples of these values include honesty, compassion, loyalty, creativity, courage, and intelligence.

Change Your Inner Dialogue

To understand and heal your inner child, it's important to listen to and assure yourself in a language that the younger version of yourself understands. Changing your inner dialogue involves tapping into a new narrative that is healing to you. It's about learning to form positive interactions with your inner child to allow them to feel safe.

You create your reality. So, the power that trauma has over you is solely in your control. When your inner dialogue is guided by trauma (cold, harsh, and damaging), you see the world from that perspective. Yet, your worldview changes when your inner dialogue is positive, hopeful, and optimistic. Your experiences inform your perception, which influences your life.

Mastering a positive inner dialogue shapes you to experience a more rewarding life. You begin to feel happier and more fulfilled. Here's how to do that:

- **Carve out time for yourself.** Taking time to be with yourself is one of the most foundational steps toward healthy dialogue. Humans generally have between 60,000 to 80,000 thoughts daily; these impact productivity (Raypole, 2022). Spending time alone allows you to shape these thoughts into more positive inner conversations. Solitude is not like isolation because it's an opportunity to recharge yourself and be enriched. Carving out time for yourself gives you a moment during a day when you are flooded with responsibility to quieten the noise and sit with yourself. Your inner child will thank you for taking this time out. You don't even need to do anything but sit and honor the silence. If you prefer, you can journal about the qualities you like about yourself and some of the things you can work on.

- **Practice gratitude.** Being grateful is one of the most potent tools against trauma. The best part is, it's free! Practicing gratitude ushers an environment for internal transformation. When you practice focusing on the good, it automatically shifts your mind out of a negative mental space and into a positive one. Simply repeating grateful statements such as "I am grateful for hot, running water each day" or "I am thankful for friends who have become family" can enrich your life. The practice of gratitude creates positive momentum in your inner dialogue. It helps you remain vibrant and not allow the bad experiences in life to rob you of the good. You can make your gratitude statement by finishing the following sentence: "I am grateful for..." As you continue to refocus your attention on good things, your energy and inner dialogue will start to take the shape of those things.

- **Avoid negative energy.** Due to the brain's negativity bias—the tendency to acknowledge adverse events easier than positive ones—it's natural to become familiar with sitting in self-pity and trauma. This bias existed as our ancient ancestors' way to survive by staying alert to danger. The mechanism isn't as needed today as it was back then. However, our mind naturally gravitates toward the negatives. That's why people can miss a beautiful sunrise by letting the day's responsibilities overshadow it. You can be so focused on what needs to be done that you forget to celebrate what has been done. Avoiding negativity involves turning away from this mentality. Stop letting the negative things overshadow the positives. Next time your mind says, "I am not good enough," decide to tell it something different. For instance, replace the negative with, "I am learning this skill and will get better at it in time." Choose to consciously observe negative thoughts when they come, but don't claim them as reality. You don't need to believe every thought you have, nor should you entertain them—especially the unbeneficial ones. Of course, you can't humanly avoid all negativity, but you can use gratitude to help you shift your focus toward the positive stuff. Doing this will have a great impact on your inner dialogue.

- **Get into affirmations.** Affirming yourself is a process that reprograms your mind to be more constructive. The word "affirm" means to declare, proclaim, or encourage something to be true. Affirmations are powerful, positive statements you can speak over your life to create a far more uplifting inner dialogue. By affirming yourself regularly, you learn to be attentive to what you want rather than focusing on what you lack. Given their value and level of importance, Chapter 8 provides more information about affirmations.

- **Practice encouraging speech and behavior.** In line with affirming yourself, start speaking kindly to your inner child. How you talk to yourself and act daily influences your inner dialogue. Practicing encouraging behavior begins with having good hygiene, dressing well, and smelling good. Let how you carry yourself be a testament to your commitment to self-growth.

- **Recognize your true nature.** Your titles, achievements, traumas, and roles are not *who you are* but *what you have.* Your true nature goes beyond what you can point out into deep internal awareness. It's easy to forget your true nature and focus on things that make you anxious. When you recognize your true nature, you feel limitless and competent. You were born with your true self, untainted by possessions and accomplishments. You live an unchained life when you get to the root of who that is.

When you avoid acknowledging your past traumas, you may open up to self-sabotaging behaviors. Internalized racism, dismissal of discrimination, alcoholism, and workaholism are all examples of this. Yet, when each individual commits to healing their inner child, these unpleasant experiences can be avoided. I believe there is a correlation between the animosity in the world and people who project their wounded inner children onto others. This, no matter the fashion, is a recipe for disaster. Healing our inner children heals generational traumas and inevitably heals the world.

Healing Trauma: Dressing Your Wounds

Healing trauma doesn't have a definite destination or final point. It's a journey that takes time, commitment, and patience. Your mind and body will always communicate what you need to heal. Social support, eating healthy, taking breaks, and doing things that bring you joy are great ways to dress your inner child's wounds. Trauma strips you away from feelings of safety and trust, so healing is all about restoring what was taken. It's about reclaiming your health, relationships, and power to live a full, rich life.

Get a Support System, Don't Isolate Yourself

Dealing with trauma can be exhausting. It's common to want to pull away from social settings and live an isolated life. However, part of self-care during trauma healing is retaining a support system. It is important to stay in touch with your friends and family. Also, stick around a community of people with the same experience. Having Black friends, for example, will also help you feel a sense of belonging. It would help if you were in spaces where you felt understood without explaining yourself. Get into a support group with other Black women with similar social and economic experiences, so you can continue to build confidence by perpetuating the pattern of belonging. The people you let around you need to be supportive and understanding, which will give you the boost you need toward healing. While isolation perpetuates feelings of trauma, getting a support system makes you feel cared for, which is integral for living beyond trauma.

Professional help can also contribute to your support system. Trauma and experiencing constant marginalization can be tiring. The frustration, fear, low moments, and challenges can take hold of your mental health when left unaddressed. So, getting a therapist involved in your healing journey is transformative. Therapy helps to organize your thoughts into concepts that make sense. You get to talk about the pressures you face as a Black woman navigating America and the spaces that come with it. Professionals help you convey these experiences in a safe space so that you can understand and process them for yourself. Not only is talking to a therapist uplifting, but you can also get advice on coping with daily experiences, specifically those that trigger you, such as microaggressive comments and behaviors.

Face It and Understand Your Power, Don't Avoid the Experience

It can be tempting to avoid dealing with traumatic events or to unpack years of trauma. However, the key ingredient to transforming trauma is to face it head-on. Permit yourself to feel and talk about your feelings as they relate to personal experiences. Take pride in being a Black woman, and find ways to address the discomfort that sometimes comes from it. Learn to be okay with your experiences and memories to move forward positively.

Facing situations also involves solving problems directly rather than letting them build up into something bigger. Little things can add up when they go unaddressed, so it's important to work through thoughts and challenges when you can. For example, if you have difficult tasks ahead of you, breaking them down into more manageable steps is a form of facing things head-on.

Get Physically Active

Physical activity is a necessary form of self-care because it helps keep your body healthy. A healthy body promotes mental wellness, which can be translated into every facet of your life. Physical well-being can relieve symptoms of depression and anxiety that can arise from constant racial discrimination and sexism. Research suggests a positive connection between physical exercise and mental health (Pedersen & Smith, 2022). Being physically active can improve your life, one movement at a time.

The benefits of physical activity include

- boosted mood

- higher confidence

- positive distraction

- improved social activity

Exercise reduces stress hormone levels and floods the body with endorphins that leave you feeling refreshed and good. It's also a great source of confidence because it helps keep your body in shape, feeling more energized, and looking more flattering. When you feel good about yourself and your body as a Black woman, you automatically aren't as affected by other people's opinions. You begin to unlearn the lie that you must walk around as the most apologetic version of yourself, and you start to accept the truth of your excellence. Exercise helps you maintain longevity and health, so you can be around to enjoy the most of your life.

Get Into a Routine

A routine is a structured and healthy way of sustaining control over your life. It refers to a series of habits and action steps that you take daily to achieve your goals. You might not always have control over the experiences and challenges you face in life, but you can control what you do daily. Getting into a routine helps you stay level-headed and maintain balance. Your routine is perhaps the only thing you can control, so make the most of it. Routines provide a structure that minimizes stress. Knowing what you will do and how helps establish purpose and consistency.

When your life lacks routine, you are more prone to mental, physical, and emotional health issues. Not having a standard daily plan can leave you feeling helpless and easily susceptible to believing harsh things about yourself. Lacking a routine leads to feelings of stress and overwhelm, which are common trauma triggers. You might find yourself self-medicating, acting out of character, or even developing some addictions due to the absence of a routine. Yet, creating a routine is a preventative measure that protects you against these things. You can keep busy but maintain balance in your life because of it. Routines help you defy that "strong Black woman" narrative by helping you manage stressors in life and plan so that you don't have to do everything in one go.

Getting into a routine provides direction and clarity in your life. You have a set time for breakfast each morning and can plan out what to eat for dinner at night. It's also a form of self-care because you can plan your morning and evening hygiene practices. Having a routine creates predictability, inspiring familiarity, safety, stability, and comfort—all signs of living beyond trauma. Staying on top of your routine simplifies life into more manageable, straightforward steps. Manageability prepares your mind to cope with unpredictable changes and builds resilience for the future.

Your routine provides you with a list of steps to follow, which increases your capacity to focus on things that matter. Going through life without the slightest plan can be overwhelming, and routines prevent this. Following a standard routine helps eliminate the need to use excessive energy and effort thinking about what needs to happen. It offers you direction that promotes the feeling of order. Routines can support other healthy habits such as good sleep, productivity, and relaxation, making it possible to be the best version of yourself despite trauma.

Consistency is a crucial part of a healthy routine. However, learning to be flexible when other things come up is also essential. Routines aren't meant to be dull or inflexible. Instead, allow some level of adjustment to happen when it's needed. Sticking to a set way of doing things, no matter how boring or draining it feels, does more harm to you than good. If you ever feel like your routine is just a loop of endless things that aren't helping you develop and care for yourself, it might be time to consider something different. Change is an inevitable and natural part of progression, so be open to adjusting your routine as often as you need to as you build toward your goals.

Celebrate Your Life

It's okay to feel joy, celebrate your successes, and bask in the goodness of your life. The media and societal stories constantly perpetuate Black pain, but there's also Black joy. You are allowed to be a happy, free Black woman. It would help if you lived your life from a place of warmth, regardless of the belief that you must carry the weight of the world. Even after trauma and discrimination, you are worthy of healing and celebration.

Enslaved Africans knew that they were not free, but they kept fighting for the possibility that you and I would be. The generations before us paved the way for our freedom, and that is something to be celebrated. Black joy is rooted in seeking the good in yourself and others. It provides positive nourishment and a safe, healing space for you. Celebrating your life is about exercising this joy. Revel in the hope that you can live a happy life because of those who came before you. Black joy requires you to rest your body, mind, and spirit after years of fighting social issues. Contrary to popular belief, you are not a victim of your circumstances but a catalyst for positive transformation. Celebrating your life rejects the ideas of discrimination, injustice, prejudice, and violence by claiming your worth as a Black person.

Caring for myself is not self-indulgence, it is self-preservation, and that is an act of political warfare. –Audre Lorde

You can shift negative narratives in your favor, and your joy honors that. You can celebrate your life by learning about your heritage and feeling proud of who you are. You can also celebrate your life by valuing your strengths as you work to improve your weaknesses. Trauma can feel compounded when race is in the mix, but you—as a Black woman—have the right to live and thrive joyfully. In the next chapter, we explore changing the narrative and breaking the negative cycles of trauma.

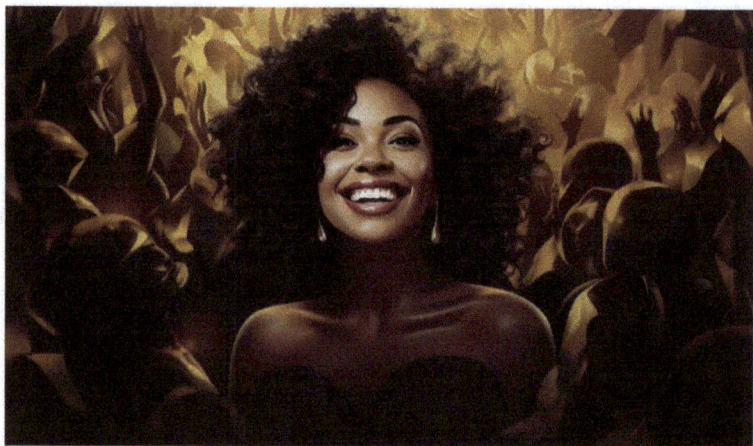

Chapter 7:

Changing the Narrative

The cycle of trauma continues until someone decides to break it, and you can be that person. The tricky part about trauma is that it interferes with our ability to care, feel safe, and build a purposeful life. You could feel trapped and not know how to lift yourself from the destruction caused by trauma. However, there's a healthy way to change the narrative. Changing your story from trauma to transformation requires a healing process to console the parts of yourself that have been hurt.

Feelings of disempowerment and disconnection are common during trauma. It's essential to work through these feelings so that you can get on the other side of them. Being empowered as someone who deals with traumatization allows you to build healthy connections with people and form new associations for yourself. Breaking the trauma cycle doesn't happen in isolation. Healing requires the basic capacities of personal agency or self-control, trust, autonomy, vulnerability, identity, and initiative (Herman, 1998). Cultivating a strong personal awareness and growing relationships helps reform these capabilities.

Trauma robs us of our sense of safety and control, but using trauma recovery steps helps restore them. For any Black woman to change the narrative of her life, she must be willing to take the pen and be the author of her own healing. People around you can only offer guidance and support, but you are the true force behind your journey. Without a personal commitment to transformation, nothing changes.

This chapter is about truly unlearning the "strong Black woman" narrative and breaking the cycle of intergenerational trauma. As African American women, we are powerful beyond measure and can use our power in soft, healing ways.

Breaking the Trauma Cycle

Newborns don't come into the world with a clean slate of emotions; we are all born with a history that starts before conception. Not only do we inherit our race, cultural background, and eye color, among other things, but we also inherit family cycles. When we are born, there's a line of stories, beliefs, and narratives tied to us. Some of what we inherit is good, while other aspects need change.

Our lineage is grounded in the profound influences of our ancestors. There's always a part of the past that lives through us, whether we feel that or not. While it's great to own our identity and continue our family story, there are also traumatic cycles that we are responsible for breaking. We are the next generation's ancestors, and just as our own forebearers laid a foundation for freedom, we must lay a positive foundation of healing. It's noble to take pride in our family stories; it's even better if we can work through some of the unresolved baggage. Trauma feels heavy, and sometimes, it might feel too overwhelming to overcome, but it is possible to heal in three trauma recovery stages.

Three Parts of Trauma Recovery

Stabilization, reprocessing, and reprogramming are three parts that guide healing trauma (Herman, 1998). The three-step trauma recovery model is based on the idea of healing as a collective and transformative process. These three parts allow for trauma-informed care, where you acknowledge the experience of trauma, realize its effects, and address what triggers you may have so that you can overcome the experience. Trauma specialists accept Dr. Judith Herman's three-step trauma healing model.

In itself, trauma adds to continued cycles of deprivation. It can contribute to poverty, jeopardize parenting, and foster attachment issues, deep distress, and instability, which can stunt growth opportunities. Fortunately, we can reduce the impact of trauma, especially generational trauma, on future descendants. Just as trauma can be passed down through generations, so too can healing. The following guides can help you change the narrative.

Stabilization

The first stage of healing trauma is stabilization, which refers to reestablishing security. It involves setting transformation goals, developing healthy coping mechanisms, and establishing safety within oneself and the environment. Focusing on providing for your basic needs, regulating yourself, and giving attention to your inner child are ways to promote stabilization. Getting adequate rest, eating well, engaging in therapy, planning, and keeping a consistent exercise regimen help to overcome symptoms of trauma.

Having a stable environment also contributes to healing trauma. For example, living in a safe place with people you trust, financial safety, freedom of movement, and support are all helpful to your journey of overcoming trauma. Recognizing the barriers you might have at this point is crucial in your healing process. Once you realize what's causing destabilization in your life, you can start to build from there.

Some examples of destabilization happening are situations like losing your home, childhood abuse, surviving domestic violence, and many others. Noticing what's harmed you works hand-in-hand with healing from it. When you feel safe and find your balance, the second part of healing begins.

Reprocessing

Now, you are better suited to tell your story and speak about your history, no matter how painful, without falling back into trauma-led patterns. Reprocessing occurs when traumatic memories turn into a part of your life that doesn't cripple you anymore. This part is about owning your past but having it lose its hold over you. Reprocessing involves remembering and grieving the trauma in a comfortable and secure environment so that you can work through it safely.

Avoiding your trauma leads to stagnation, but reprocessing helps to prevent this and gets you on track toward growth. It allows you to accept your reality and live beyond the issues that have impacted it. A therapist can provide a confidential, secure space for you to process your story. It's your choice to recount what you feel and how it's manifesting in your life. Your therapist plays a significant role in helping you navigate the second stage of healing trauma. Therapists become allies to you and supporters of your growth. As you slowly open up and share the fragments of your experiences, your therapist helps to bring those into a more clear, healing image. Therapy allows you to give a verbal account of your emotions and events to contextualize and understand them and yourself better. Reprocessing doesn't only look at the traumatic events in your life but also your response to them. It's also a chance to assess the responses of the people in your life.

Having an in-depth understanding, through talk therapy, of how trauma has manifested in your life helps resolve feelings of guilt and shame associated with it. During this process, what contributes to long-lasting joy is the ability to form deep relationships, which are easier to form when you grow to trust yourself. The acceptance you go through from reprocessing affirms your choice to heal from the past, but it doesn't excuse what happened. Your story and experience are still valid; reprocessing empowers you to claim your power from them.

The stage of reprocessing trauma never really ends. New conflicts and challenges arise daily that inevitably trigger trauma and possibly bring new aspects to light. However, as you continue to be patient with yourself and commit to reprocessing your trauma, you begin to find ways to cope. With a commitment to the process, you'll notice yourself reclaiming your history with renewed hope and energy. This will bring a new fire into how you engage with life. Eventually, things that used to be triggering will no longer keep you stuck; healing will come, and time will move again. After repeatedly processing your triggers in a safe space and talking about painful experiences, they will no longer arouse strong emotions. Your traumas then become a part of your life but do not have a hold on it. Once reprocessing is done, the trauma that used to affect your present experiences begins to feel like the distant past. At this point, your triggers are few and far between.

Reprogramming

Reprogramming is the third stage of healing, whereby you use the insight you've gained from the first two steps to become the best version of yourself. It is the process of integrating your past (the acceptance of personal trauma) with your present life (the healing from or reprocessing of it), so you can fully reconnect to yourself. The fewer your triggers become, the deeper into the reprogramming stage you go.

At this point, it's common to regain trust and confidence in yourself again. You also begin to feel trust in people with better insight into what's good for you and what's not. By the reprogramming stage, you start to feel more comfortable setting boundaries. Reprogramming pushes you to take the initiative over your life. You begin to process your identity as a Black woman as more than a traumatic experience. Reprogramming prepares you to see life from a positive, fresh perspective and build strong connections. You can start to pull away from connections that confirm the false reality of yourself. For example, people who mistreat you or aren't aligned with your healing path can slowly fall away. Your life opens up to the possibility of greater intimacy and development.

To combat the trauma you've carried for so long, your capacities for self-care and self-soothing need to be reconstructed. That's where the three steps come in. Stabilization, reprocessing, and reprogramming can be part of both individual and group therapies to help you overcome. Doing this journey with people with similar understandings and stories also encourages and strengthens coping mechanisms.

Different Therapy Options for Trauma Relief

The three steps for healing inform many therapies. Everyone responds differently to trauma, and it's important to know the various approaches you can take toward healing. Options give you a chance to decide what works for you:

- **Cognitive behavioral therapy (CBT):** CBT is often considered the first line of defense. It helps you identify unhelpful thought patterns and learn how to cope with adversity. For example, CBT replaces negative thoughts ("I am not enough") with positive thoughts ("I have a lot to contribute") and behaviors.

- **Prolonged exposure (PE) therapy:** This form of therapy involves bringing up trauma-related feelings, memories, and situations to face the fears head-on rather than avoid them. For example, if you've survived a horrific car accident and developed a fear of cars, your therapy could guide you to safely engage with this fear by spending time around and in a car. Over time, the fear will lessen due to constant confrontation of it.

- **Eye movement desensitization and reprocessing (EMDR):** Sessions are conducted with a professional to help you transform thought patterns and directly focus on the memory of trauma to process and let go of it. I've done EMDR before, and it often involves talking while allowing your eyes to follow a light that travels left to right in front of you. This opens up both sides of your brain.

- **Narrative therapy:** This process of retelling your story from an uplifting perspective empowers you to change your perspective of yourself and the world (*Narrative Therapy Methods*, 2024). For example, a therapist can prompt you to retell a story about your trauma, first from your experience, then by changing the characters in the story so that you can see it more objectively. After that, you'll be asked to name the problem by pointing to one or more elements of the story and discussing how it makes you feel. Retelling your story is an approach therapists use to help you separate the experience from your identity. It's a reminder that you are not your trauma.

- **Art and music therapy:** Various forms of creative expression are introduced during these therapy sessions to encourage emotional processing and trauma healing. For example, you might draw an image or create a sound to represent how you feel inside. Art and music therapy are different ways of identifying and communicating your emotions.

- **Psychodynamic therapy:** To understand what motivates certain behaviors, this therapy aims to improve self-awareness about the effects the past has on your present. Perhaps, you might notice yourself avoiding certain environments, even at the expense of being late to work, not realizing that you do this because they trigger you. Psychodynamic therapy helps to identify these patterns and change them.

- **Somatic therapy:** This process uncovers how emotions from trauma can affect the body. Trauma is stored as tension in your body, and the process of releasing it is somatic therapy. For example, without much talking, you would sit with a therapist and safely process the physical experiences of your trauma. It's a way to permit your body to remember how trauma impacted it.

You and your therapist can combine various options to create a healthy treatment plan. Trauma-informed therapies help treat and heal the underlying effects of past experiences.

Complementary Therapy Alternatives

While the trauma therapies above are valuable, trauma therapists also support engaging in other complementary alternatives (Lebow, 2021). Having additional options at your disposal helps enrich your healing journey:

- **Acupuncture:** This is a traditional Chinese practice of penetrating the skin with metallic needles in gentle and specific movements. Please, don't be turned off by this practice because of the needles. I do it, and you can barely feel it, honestly. Once the needles are positioned, you can lay there and meditate. I find it extremely relaxing and beneficial.

- **Meditation:** This exercise invites calmness and mindful presence into your life. Try downloading any one of the popular mindfulness apps on your phone; some good ones include Headspace, Calm, and Breethe. Use these to participate in a roughly five-minute calming meditation daily.

- **Tai chi:** This is a martial arts exercise that engages a range of movements to promote flexibility, balance, and strength to achieve rest and ease. Try a YouTube channel for on-demand lessons. You will notice the emotional and physical benefits right away.

- **Yoga:** Yoga is a mind-body practice that reduces stress and encourages emotional processing. It is a great opportunity to find your people, get in shape, and connect your mind and body; it helps to promote healing.

Further recommendations to help you process trauma daily include utilizing breathing techniques, relaxation strategies, and aerobic exercises. Trauma needs to be processed both emotionally and physically since it impacts every aspect of well-being.

Relaxation Strategies to Relieve Trauma Anxiety

Life can get busy and help us avoid thinking about trauma. However, when things slow down, the memories can creep back up into our minds. When we go to sleep at night, experiences can resurface. All this discomfort can increase restlessness and trauma anxiety; relaxation strategies can help mitigate this.

Progressive Muscle Relaxation

Muscle relaxation helps to manage stress. Whether you feel overwhelmed or in control of your emotions, you can benefit from practicing relaxation. Progressive muscle relaxation helps you slowly release tension across your body. Each muscle group gets special attention to help you be more tuned in to physical sensations and potential parts that need relaxation.

To start practicing some muscle relaxation, you can do the following:

1. Tense your toes for five seconds, and relax them.

2. Notice the sensations that come with tensing and relaxing.

3. Gradually work your way up your body, tensing and relaxing each muscle group.

4. Tense your neck and shoulders for five seconds and then relax.

5. Notice the sensation that comes from doing that.

6. Relax for 30 seconds, then repeat.

This relaxation technique is a simple way to relieve tension and find an effective method to de-stress during demanding days. In moments of distress, visualize peace taking over your body. Continuously practicing this technique will help you establish calmness, especially in the face of adversity.

Guided Imagery

Guided imagery is an effective stress reliever. It is a process that stimulates calmness of the mind and body through vivid daydreaming or visualization. Typically, the process is directed by a qualified instructor through recordings or in person.

You can follow these steps to exercise guided imagery in the comfort of your space:

1. Get into a comfortable position. You can lie down, recline your chair, or sit in a cross-legged position.

2. Get rid of distractions. Ensure you are in a relaxing space. For example, if you are practicing this exercise at home, be sure to switch off the television and turn off your phone's notifications, so you can get the most out of your practice.

3. Breathe deeply. Use your breath to center yourself throughout the process. You are welcome to close your eyes and focus on taking deep breaths in and out. As you inhale, let your stomach expand, and then, allow it to contract with every exhalation. You might notice your shoulders rising and falling as you breathe, which can signal tension in your body.

4. Vividly envision yourself relaxing all the tension. Use your imagination to feel yourself float above the stress with each inhalation and exhalation. Picturing yourself at a happy place or simply creating one in your mind can help release tension. For example, choose to prompt your mind to remember the most enjoyable memory. It could be a trip to your favorite theme park or walks on the beach. Think about how happy it makes you to be there. Focus on the different smells, textures, feelings, and other great qualities from this memory or imaginary scenario.

5. Get into detail. Think about each detail of this visualization. Try to involve your senses. Consider what the space looks like: Is there sun? Is the sky blue? Is it crowded? Is it loud? Engaging your senses will help this image feel more natural to you.

6. Stay calm, and enjoy yourself. Have fun with the image. Let yourself feel at peace and refreshed.

The objective is to tap into your powerful innermost voice and creativity. Productive use of imagination is at the center of this practice. Guided imagery can be practiced in different ways, and it can be experienced in therapy or yoga practices.

Box Breathing

Also referred to as square breathing, box breathing is a breathwork technique that involves deep breathing. It slows down your breathing to get more from the practice. Box breathing distracts your mind, calms your nervous system, and decreases anxiety in your body. The technique itself is simple but highly effective and powerful.

With any breathwork, it's important to find a quiet and comfortable place to sit. Pull up a chair, or place a pillow on the ground to get comfortable. Put one hand on your chest and the other on your stomach. If you sit on a chair, be sure your back is supported, and your feet are firm on the ground.

Continue to breathe as you usually would. Do this for a minute. Take account of how breathing feels typically. If your chest rises but your stomach doesn't, there's an issue we call "shallow breathing" because you aren't getting the full benefits of drawing deeper breaths. It's correctable, though, and many of us do it without noticing. If you are shallow breathing, consciously get yourself to inhale in a manner that helps your stomach rise as your lungs fill with oxygen. Now, notice the difference in your breathing from making the change.

Once your body feels prepared to breathe intentionally, it's a good opportunity to transition into box breathing.

Here are four valuable steps to help you get started:

1. Take a deep inhalation(see your stomach rising), slowing your breathing for four counts. Acknowledge the feeling of your body filling with oxygen.

2. Pause once your lungs reach air capacity and you can no longer keep inhaling. Think of this as a break at the top

of your inhalation. At the pause, hold your breath for four counts. Avoid inhaling or exhaling during the hold.

3. After four counts, slowly release the breath by exhaling gradually from pursed lips. As you exhale from your mouth, make sure it is slow and that you can feel each bit of air leaving your body.

4. Relax at the bottom of your breath as you recognize there's no more air to breathe out. Finally, repeat these steps until you feel realigned, calm, and connected with yourself.

If you battle to do four-second counts, feel free to adjust to two or three seconds, so your practice is tailored to your needs. Make sure that you remain comfortable throughout your healing journey so that you can stay focused on the things that bring more hope and positivity into your life. The aim is to remain connected to yourself and never stop honoring your mind-body needs.

To change your narrative, you can repeat these exercises as often as you need. A short 30 seconds to a minute of purposeful relaxation will leave you feeling more self-aware, calm, and in control of yourself as well as your behaviors. In the long run, relaxation techniques will save you energy as they provide clarity about what is worth your effort and what isn't.

Mindfulness Exercise: Connect Your Senses

Changing your narrative is all about connecting to the true self. It allows you to live an authentic life beyond the trauma-painted lens that the world views you through. Mindfulness exercises work together with relaxation techniques to invite centeredness into your life.

Here's how you can practice mindfulness:

1. Firmly place your feet on the ground while maintaining a comfortable sitting position. Place your hands on your thighs, and maintain an unforced upright posture.

2. Pause and direct your focus to your physical sensations. Pay attention to the feeling of your feet on the ground: How does it feel? Is it cold? Are you comfortable? Do your feet have any aches?

3. Now, gently move your attention away from your feet to the feeling of your butt on the seat. Notice any comfort or discomfort that you are feeling.

4. Continue to drive your focus from the seat and your body on it up toward your spine. Pay attention to whether your body is resting on the chair or slightly off it. How does that feel? What sensations are being created?

5. Pay attention to the feeling of your clothes against your body. Are they loose or tight-fitting? Do you feel comfortable? Is the material soft or coarse?

6. Gradually bring more attention to your senses. What sounds can you hear around you? What can you see? What can you touch?

7. Close your eyes, and continue to process your physical sensations. Bring your attention back to how your skin feels today. Are you hot or cold? Is the air around you cool? Can you feel your hair sway a little?

8. Notice your breathing. Pay attention to the feeling of inhaling and exhaling.

9. When you are ready, open your eyes before continuing with your day.

Exercising mindfulness is about taking inventory of everything, one thing at a time, in the present moment. It's about bringing your attention to what you have at your disposal right now and also how your body and mind are feeling and reacting in the moment. The aim of this body scan meditation is to recognize your sensations, so you aren't distracted by worry or anxiety about things you can't control. Mindfulness increases your capacity to notice the present and immerse yourself in the experiences in front of you.

As African American women, we face a lot of challenges and confrontations across various areas of our lives. Learning ways to keep ourselves grounded in moments that threaten to bring us out of our peace is helpful. Our level-headedness and calm spirit set us apart in positive ways when being tested by things or people.

My dear Black sister, you gain nothing from letting the world get the best of you. Relaxation techniques can help you stabilize your mind and body so that you can manage whatever comes your way. Using these techniques promotes a sense of stillness that can help you overcome difficulties without denying your emotions and humanity in the process.

Change the Narrative: Tips to Help You Overcome the "Strong Black Woman" Stereotype

In the spirit of breaking the trauma cycle and changing the narrative, it's essential to redefine your idea of strengths as a Black woman. Of the Black population in the US, women make up 52%, with over 21 million of us (Fleming, n.d.-a). Yet, in the US, as a whole, Black women only make up just over 13% of the population (*Women of Color in the United States (Quick Take)*, 2023). The Black women within our communities are expected to be the glue and source of nurture. We are also considered strong because we are a minority—the 13%; so, without our resilience, the world threatens to chew us up. However, we are also human beings; neither of these statistics considers that. While we are expected to stand tall and hide our emotions, we can lose some of our humanity.

It's okay if, like me, you are tired of being the "strong Black woman." It's okay if you want to be more than this stereotype if you, like myself, would like to be comforted when you're upset or asked what you need occasionally. You are allowed to embrace your personality, thoughts, and feelings without the pressure to conform to this narrative. Trust me, having a bad day and admitting when you need help doesn't undermine how capable you are. Just because you can carry the world on your shoulders as a descendant of ancestors who proved that possible, doesn't mean you should subject yourself to that burden.

The strong Black woman stereotype portrays us as people who don't put up with nonsense from others. We hold people accountable for their actions and stand firm in our ethics and values. The image is constantly of us having to endure tough situations and holding it together for the sake of everyone else. Yet, this isn't sustainable or healthy. Being strong shouldn't mean sidelining our own needs or sacrificing our well-being for someone else's. Whether we realize it or not, being held to this unrealistic standard prevents us from taking care of ourselves.

Changing the narrative is about striking a balance between strength and care. You can be proud to be a Black woman who can hold up her family and friends while admitting when you need the same courtesy extended to you. Don't allow yourself to be trapped within a stereotype that keeps you from being kind, gentle, and good to yourself.

Tip One: Permit Yourself to Feel

You deserve to have your feelings and thoughts, no matter how other people feel or think about them. Your strength doesn't need to undermine your vulnerability, and you can do and be both. As a Black woman, you deserve to feel supported and cared for without restriction.

Tip Two: Ask for Help When You Need It

Being courageous enough to ask for help is true strength. You are not weak or incompetent for needing assistance from time to time—everyone does. Asking for help when you need it conveys a sense of self-awareness and sincerity that hiding your true feelings doesn't. Even when it feels uncomfortable, asking for help is a good starting point for overcoming the strong Black woman stereotype. If anything, receiving assistance from others fuels resilience and keeps you on the healthier side of the "strong" scale.

Tip Three: Embrace Vulnerability

Asking for help is a part of vulnerability, and the rest is about expressing how you feel. Sharing your thoughts with others can provide clarity while helping you feel supported. When your vulnerability is received, it can help you feel validated, seen, heard, and cared for. It's a reminder that your voice and opinions matter. Whether you are embracing your vulnerability with friends and family or your therapist, getting things off your chest unburdens you.

Tip Four: Practice Self-Care

Self-care is foundational to changing the narrative. Practicing self-care is about permitting yourself to feel supported and nurtured. It involves surrounding yourself with people who empower you and provide a sense of belonging—people you can share experiences with and not have to hide yourself in the process. Self-care is about having fun, doing enjoyable things, and cherishing every moment of your life. Some examples of self-care include quality time with friends, solo time, hiking, running a warm bubble bath, or taking a few minutes to do relaxation exercises. You are worthy of care, and what better way to start receiving it than to make it a standard for yourself? You deserve it.

Tip Five: Release Other People's Expectations of You

Being a strong person is a good thing, but true strength comes from recognizing the importance of vulnerability too. Release the longstanding expectation that you can only choose one or the other. You aren't bound to the pre-existing definition of a strong Black woman. Change the narrative by creating healthy expectations for yourself and letting go of the ones that are preset for you. Be confident in your choices, and be a Black woman who can have it all.

Becoming more confident in your identity as a Black woman requires you to take care of yourself. As you do, you'll begin to feel less pressured to conform to other people's unrealistic standards of who you should be. You'll notice yourself begin to lead with compassion, empathy, and kindness as you exercise both strength and vulnerability. The next chapter considers how you can use this newfound self-care and love to affirm yourself as the lovely Black woman you are.

Chapter 8:

Self-Affirmations

A lot of us battle negative thoughts from time to time. Negative thoughts can impact our confidence and mood, together with reducing productivity. When we are constantly beating ourselves up, it can be difficult to find the good in life. It can also make it hard to cherish the wonderful moments in our lives because we persistently hear the negative inner voice criticize us. The issue with inner criticism is that it eventually turns into self-fulfilling narratives. It can be tough to separate ourselves from these thoughts as we take them as truth. The more we think about something, the higher the likelihood of us believing it over time. Negative thinking can significantly restrict our growth, hold back our careers, and deteriorate our relationships. Luckily, negative thoughts and beliefs can be transformed through affirmations.

Part of dressing the wounds of trauma is speaking positively to yourself; that's where affirmations come in. These refer to helpful statements to overcome self-sabotaging, negative inner dialogue. Affirming yourself daily is a great way to combat negative thoughts that creep into your mind. You might think, *I wish I could stick up for myself more in social settings instead of cowering during confrontations.* A thought like this can break you down, making it hard to face life with zeal. However, when you use personal affirmations, you replace that negative thought with something more uplifting. For example, the negative thought can be replaced with, *I find it hard to speak up sometimes, but I can change that*, or simply, *I am learning to self-advocate.* Self-affirmations remind you that you can do the things that your mind tells you you can't.

Affirmations drive positivity and can improve your life greatly. This chapter covers the power of affirmations. It also highlights affirmations specifically designed for trauma recovery and Black women. Additionally, the chapter provides space to create self-affirmations that you can use daily to help you on your healing journey.

The Power of Self-Affirmations

Trauma negatively shifts your perspective of yourself and the world around you. Self-affirmations are a way to unburden yourself from the lies that trauma has told. Affirmations allow you to replace an anxious thought with a helpful one. For example, *I am terrible at this. Maybe, I should stop trying,* is replaced with, *I am new to this, but I will learn the skill with more practice.* Introducing relevant affirmations into your life is beneficial, particularly ones that focus on your personal experience and help you heal.

The science behind affirmations suggests that they eventually transform how your mind works. Neuroplasticity is the brain's ability to adapt to different situations in life and change to help you understand things from a different perspective (Raypole, 2020). When you practice self-affirmations, you take full advantage of neuroplasticity. Without seeing it, you gently guide your mind to think, process, and adapt to situations more positively. This is not only a mood booster but also improves your problem-solving ability and managing stressful circumstances. What's more, affirmations can ease mental health concerns such as low self-esteem, depression, anxiety, and other conditions. The brain regions stimulated by affirmations have a positive ripple effect on well-being and one's outlook.

You can use affirmations in multiple situations where you want to inspire transformation. For example, you could recite an affirmation (or two) to calm your nerves before a big meeting. You can also repeat positive statements to improve motivation and overcome bad habits. Affirmations can be more effective when you pair them with practical actions. For instance, use relaxation techniques and positive statements to start your day. Also, write little reminders and stick them in visible places around your home in your workspace so that you are regularly reminded of positive thoughts. Other practical actions can include aligning your affirmations with goals that you want to achieve.

Affirmations don't work if you don't say them with an expectation and desire for healing. To make self-affirmations more effective, it's helpful to set them in the present by starting your statements with the phrase "I am." This indicates things happening now, which makes it easier for your mind to believe them. In the same way that you can speak negatively, saying, "I am so bad at this," you can speak positively by saying, "I am learning this." It's important to keep your affirmations real, relatable, and relevant. Ensure that you prioritize affirming yourself daily. Include affirmation time in your routine, so you don't go a day without speaking power into your life. Committing to self-affirmations will reframe your mind over time. Eventually, your brain will gravitate toward replacing negative thoughts with positivity without you consciously pulling them out. With practice, healthy patterns become natural responses.

Affirmations for Trauma Recovery

Positive statements typically target areas in your life that need transformation. For example, if healing is the goal, you need to create or find affirmations that speak to your healed version. If you feel unworthy, the first affirmation to include in your list is "I am worthy." Affirmations are supposed to counteract negative thoughts and bring more positivity into your space.

Along with the other techniques listed in this book, affirmations can help you live beyond your trauma. Affirming yourself to overcome trauma is a way to remember how powerful of a Black woman you are without feeling the need to project "strength." The things that have happened to you don't define who you are, but your response to them does. The techniques that you combine, along with your affirmations, help to transform trauma into purpose. Your healing starts with you speaking the good into your life and acting it out. The affirmations don't heal trauma, and they support you in doing that.

Here's a list of affirmations you can use for trauma recovery:

- I am worthy.

- I am allowed to feel.

- I am allowed to speak up for what I believe in.

- I am supported.

- My trauma does not define me.

- What happened was not my fault.

- I deserve to live unapologetically.

- It's okay to be the way I am right now.

- I understandably felt the way I did.

- I understandably did the things I did to cope with my experience.

- I understandably didn't know how to do better at that time.

- My unhealthy habits were survival mechanisms to protect myself.

- I am not intentionally self-sabotaging; it's my brain's way of trying to protect me.

- I can build new, healthy habits because I am not in danger anymore.

- I am safe.

- I don't need permission to exist.

- I am not my trauma.

- My flaws are not a measurement of my worth or capabilities.

- It's okay to have a bad day, week, or month; healing is not a straight line.

- I fall and bounce back up again.

- Breathe!

- This is passing through me.

- I choose to be gentle with myself.

- I acknowledge my feelings without explaining or justifying what I feel.

These affirmations are a starting point; feel free to expand on this list and add more personal and specific statements for yourself. Remember, affirmations act as rewards for your brain, boosting your emotional and physical well-being. Since you can use affirmations for trauma, you can also create some for self-empowerment.

Affirmations for Every Black Woman

Dear Black woman, you are more than your trauma, which means your affirmations need to speak to who you are as well. Don't just create positive statements for your healing but also for your upliftment.

Your affirmations not only serve to encourage you but also permit you to thrive in your skin freely. What's better is that you are validating yourself, so your nervous system begins to recognize your voice as the one to respond to. The more you affirm yourself as a Black woman, the more distance you create between yourself and the need to be validated by other people. Some great affirmations to get you going include:

- I step into my power today and every day.

- I breathe life into my dreams.

- I exhale anxiety and welcome peace.

- I release any lack of reciprocity.

- I protect my energy.

- My discipline is rewarded.

- I bring a palpable energy into every room.

- The opinions and perceptions of others do not define me.

- Shame is not my fate; I choose joy, playfulness, and self-acceptance.

- I acknowledge my inner child and step closer to healing.

- I focus on my needs and ensure they are met.

- I am clear about what I want and the direction of my desires.

- My Black power, excellence, and magic speak for themselves.

- I am a soft, intelligent Black woman.

- I do not apologize for my joy, even when it makes others uncomfortable.

Setting your affirmations as a Black woman can empower you to stand tall in a world that prefers you to shrink. Speaking positively to yourself inspires a sense of clarity about who you are, and that's something the world can't take from you. Reminding yourself of your value, contributions, and worth is important because external systems won't stop long enough to do it for you.

Also, creating affirmations for yourself can prepare you to face adversity when confronted by it. You'll be less likely to internalize hurtful things like racism and sexism when you speak truth to power through affirmations daily. When you allow yourself to walk out of your home knowing exactly who you are and what you bring to the table, you simply become less bothered by someone else's inability to see your value. Though biases and barriers will still exist, affirmations will breathe new life into you. Your positive statements will encourage you to define your strengths and sharpen your capabilities to overcome these barriers.

Self-affirmations will help you realize that your existence, story, and voice are important. These three things are a testament to the progress you have made and continue to make. Your desires as a Black woman are achievable, and you gain that understanding through positive statements. Generations of leaders and unapologetic individuals paved the way for you to feel empowered to reach your goals.

Tips to Use Affirmations Effectively

Developing effective affirmations will help you achieve the transformation you want for yourself. When used effectively, affirmations are a great self-help tool. The benefits of your daily affirmations depend on how you use them. Let's explore how you can start.

Lean Toward Personal Affirmations

Nowadays, there are affirmations everywhere. Positive statements are traded in bulk through commercial and other platforms. For example, social media is filled with stock affirmations. You'll find "positive vibes" on t-shirts, in blogs, and as motivational images on social feeds—that's just the beginning. There's no harm in getting on the bandwagon and enjoying these affirmations, but creating personal ones that address your needs is essential. When you have personal affirmations, you become more determined to work on them. It also helps to link affirmations to your core values. For example, honesty, integrity, and commitment are great guiding points.

Personal affirmations are effective because they speak to what matters to you. Instead of recycling what the world shares, you get to talk directly about what you are experiencing. For instance, if you feel down on yourself about your career not being as rewarding as you'd hoped, counter these negative emotions with a positive reminder. You might want to create a personal affirmation that speaks to this situation along the lines of, "I am capable of growth and learning in any environment."

Constructing an affirmation such as this one serves as a reminder of the positive reason why your job is worth continuing with. Other reminders in this scenario are that your job provides for your lifestyle and that you might have lovely coworkers who are worth considering. It's important to keep your mind glued to the good things, no matter how challenging the situation might seem.

Stay True to Yourself, Walk the Talk

Keeping your affirmations relevant to your experiences is a way of staying true to yourself. Affirmations are most effective when centered around values, goals, and believable statements. However, they shouldn't just stop there; you need to walk the talk as well. Part of staying true to yourself is putting action behind your words. Change is only possible when you move beyond statements into practicing what you say.

For example, if you feel out of shape, you might create an affirmation that allows you to see your body from a positive perspective. However, updating your wardrobe to include items that fit you better or incorporating exercises to help you feel and look your best can help the affirmation be more effective. When you can look in the mirror and feel confident in what you're wearing, it helps your brain to accept that what's underneath that outfit is also beautiful. Likewise, when you get physically active, you begin to feel healthy enough that you believe it when you say an affirmation. Telling yourself something positive like, "I cherish my body and appreciate what it does for me," is more engaging when you work out, eat well, exercise regularly, and care for yourself. Staying true to yourself involves being accountable to your affirmations by acting in ways that confirm them.

Be Specific

Affirmations that are centered around your traits can help you see yourself positively. You have unique traits, and you can use affirmations effectively by highlighting those traits. For example, be specific about what you see in yourself by saying, "I am kind," "My smile is beautiful," and "I treat myself with compassion daily." These statements work better than the more ultra-positive ones that aren't specific. Examples of ultra-positive affirmations include "I am beautiful," and "I love myself." Such statements seem to be less effective in inspiring long-term change than more specific ones (Raypole, 2020).

Practice Affirmations Regularly

Making a daily commitment to affirming yourself can transform your life. To get the most from self-affirmation, you need to be consistent and practice it frequently so that your brain experiences constant exposure.

For a more regular practice of affirmations, you can consider the following things:

- Start slow and make a schedule. Set out three to five minutes twice a day to practice your affirmations. Perhaps, you can say a few affirmations in the morning after you wake up. Then, say another set in the evening before bed.

- Be persistent. You can repeat your affirmations at least 10 times each day. Hear what you are saying, and pay attention to what you feel after saying it. Speak your affirmations aloud as someone confident in what's being said.

- Get someone to help you stay true to yourself. A friend or someone you trust can help you reinforce positivity. Ask a friend to listen as you recite affirmations. Hopefully, the person you trust will encourage you, so these become more believable to you.

- Be consistent. It's important to commit to your daily schedule for positivity; so, don't skip days. If you want, you can incorporate your affirmations into your workout, relaxation practices, and any other things that you do during the day. Incorporating them into an already existing routine can promote consistency.

- Be patient. Most importantly, be compassionate and patient with yourself because anything new takes time to master. You might forget or miss a day or two, but keep on trying. Your patience and persistence will create a habit of affirmation. It's well documented that it takes 21 days to form a habit; let today be day 1 of your new way of thinking.

Regularly practicing affirmations helps the positive statements to translate into habits. Now that you have some tips to help you on your journey get ready to create personal affirmations.

Interactive Part 3: Create Personal Affirmations

By creating personal affirmations, you can ensure that you say things that will benefit your life the most. Your affirmations are a significant step toward self-improvement; taking them seriously and being intentional will benefit you greatly. From the information in this chapter, create your affirmations; you can list five to start. Use the following prompts to inspire you and build from there.

Write one or more affirmations that your inner child needs to hear today.

_____

_____

_____

Write one or more affirmations that address the beauty of your vulnerability as a Black woman.

_____

_____

_____

Write one or more affirmations for yourself to read tomorrow morning.

Chapter 9:

Live Your Life Beyond Trauma

It's traumatic to hear stories of slavery and the mistreatment of Black people that have been happening for centuries. Even worse, the trauma is perpetuated by the reality that racial issues and oppression are still prevalent today. When you feel you can't catch a break because Black people are always put against a wall or pitted against each other, it can deplete your emotional cup. Watching videos or reading about people who look like you being shot, beaten, and killed daily is also retraumatizing. And for the sake of your mental health, it's important to learn how to be upset that these things are happening but not be consumed by that rage. You need to learn to live life beyond your trauma because that's where your freedom and emotional healing lie.

In previous chapters, you learned about trauma, unpacked its effects, and engaged with strategies to help you transform it. With those tools, you can now immerse yourself in a life that's empowered and free from the weight of trauma. You get to live your life beyond trauma and truly practice being "more than your trauma." Daily practices such as relaxation techniques and affirmations are the stepping stones to living this life of transformation and healing.

You may have held onto trauma for the majority of your life, but that can change now. It's time for you to live a life that breaks free of the things that have kept you stuck, and this chapter is a guide to how.

Daily Living: How to Cope With Racial Tension and Trauma

Racism and racist incidents can be huge triggers for a Black woman in any part of the world. It's important to identify a set of coping tools to help you overcome these recurring moments and keep your peace during these experiences while self-advocating for respect and demanding change from the systems at large. Without effective coping mechanisms, the stress of discrimination and racial prejudice can accumulate tension in your life. This can turn into chronic trauma that is overwhelming to deal with, especially if you don't have a strong support system.

However, there are ways to cope with racial tension and trauma. At the same time, you can develop a community to help you during this time. Since your experiences as an African American can be overwhelming, it's beneficial to do your best to establish a safe environment for yourself. It's also helpful to start processing your experiences in ways that make you feel seen, accepted, and appreciated—if not by others, then by yourself.

Validate Your Reality

Feeling like the racial tension and trauma in your life is your fault is a common, unfortunate experience. But you aren't at fault. Nothing is wrong with you, and you don't have to act strong when you are hurt by it. Racism is a form of trauma that's very real, especially for us Black women who experience it daily. Whether it's through implicit actions or overt behaviors, on an individual scale or an institutionalized system, our reality is valid. What you feel about racial trauma is real, so it matters, regardless of how often you are told to suck it up or get over it.

To validate your reality, you need to honor your emotions. Stop waiting for other people to see how bad racism is. Instead, be true to your intuition. If someone makes you feel targeted or your intuition tells you that something isn't right, trust it. You are your biggest guardian and shouldn't need anyone else to validate your experiences. Relying on external forces for validation can create anxiety and confusion. It can make you question your experiences, destabilize your emotions, and make you feel like you need to live an apologetic life. What's more, it can reduce self-confidence and cause you to make avoidable mistakes and have issues focusing on what matters.

Relying on others to make you feel good or accept your experiences is not beneficial. When you do rely on external factors, you permit your circumstances to dictate your perspective. This can make it difficult to trust your thoughts, feelings, and judgments about your experiences. An assumption is created that the experience isn't what it is, or you are "overthinking" what's happening. Invalidating your experiences of racial trauma can make you feel needy, even though you aren't. Yet, self-validation can make you feel more assured and notice that your experiences are worth backing up.

Validating your reality includes

- affirming yourself.

- listening to your inner child.

- prioritizing what you need.

- accepting your mistakes.

- changing negative thoughts to self-affirming ones.

- being kind to yourself.

- noticing your feelings and accepting them.

- acknowledging your vulnerability and not feeling the need to be "strong."

- celebrating your effort, progress, and successes.

- recognizing and living in Black joy.

You deserve to be supported, regardless of how the world feels about it. If you feel someone is being racist or discriminatory toward you, don't question it. Also, don't allow external factors to manipulate your reality. Instead, it would help if you learned to validate yourself. Other people's validation should be a bonus confirming what you already know, but it is not the only thing you rely on.

Most importantly, the racial tension and trauma you experience in your life do not determine who you are. So, you don't deserve to feel like an outcast in your own space. Also, you don't have to process this trauma alone.

Speak Openly About Your Experience

In the spirit of not doing this journey alone, you need to find a trusted person or community of people with whom you can speak openly. Your experience matters, and having a community to share it with will enrich it more. Speaking openly about your experience always allows you to have honest and genuine conversations about issues that impact you. For example, you might find it beneficial to speak about racism, ethnicity, history, generational trauma, and things you need support for.

Having friends or being with family that you can talk to about issues that impact you helps you to decompress. It also helps to validate your reality beyond what you already know. In sharing, feel free to ask if the people you talk to need any support from you as well. Topics about racism and discrimination can be heavy, so it's also good to check whether people are in a good place to talk about them. Speaking openly can help you all reflect on individual experiences and exchange different ideas on how to cope with them.

Separate Who You Are From What Is Happening to You

The negative impacts of much racial trauma can be mitigated through identity affirmation. This is the process of talking with your therapist about your struggles to help you recognize false perspectives or internalized beliefs about your life and yourself (Krouse, n.d.). Identity affirmation enables you to separate who you are from the negative experiences you are confronted with. It exposes who you are, what you value, and the thoughts that work for you, which helps overcome negative thinking and messages perpetuated by society.

Separate yourself from the negativity to re-solidify self-care, love, and compassion. Some questions you can consider asking yourself to affirm your identity are

- How do I find beauty in who I am?

- What is important to me?

- How do I honor my values?

Separating who you are from what's happening helps you define your identity without being influenced by the racist comments you encounter. It's like rewriting the narrative about yourself truthfully and lovingly.

Reclaim Your Time and Space

Identifying who you are and what matters to you gives you the opportunity to reclaim your power, time, and space. It's good to take some time to get the distance and rest you need from trauma experiences. You deserve to reclaim your identity and recover. Taking your control back through reclaiming your time and space is a way to heal racial trauma. It's also a way to reignite self-love in a world that's constantly trying to block you from it.

Avoid Doom-Scrolling

If being on social media is something that causes you anxiety from time to time, it's good to take breaks from it. Doom-scrolling is the act of aimlessly scrolling on social media and the news, which can be overwhelming with negative news and content (Deering, 2023). An overload of this information can create internal frustrations that reinforce trauma. Nothing can normalize watching your community of people be violated, dehumanized, and brutalized. If anything, doom-scrolling adds to mental health conditions and racial trauma.

Looking through content that makes you feel down on yourself or increases anxiety about your racial identity is counterproductive. Avoiding doom-scrolling is important because you don't need to witness every piece of news out there, especially information that can cause you emotional and mental harm. It's okay to choose not to watch reels and videos of Black people getting brutalized on the streets because these are traumatizing. Contrary to the popularized belief, you are allowed to create some distance between yourself and current affairs when it damages or threatens your health. You aren't letting anyone down by avoiding doom-scrolling, nor is it an act of denying what's happening around you. Your experience as a Black woman will still be your truth. You don't need to doom-scroll in an attempt to validate it. Protecting your mental health is paramount, even if it means you aren't a part of every movement or looking at every racially motivated post.

Take Action: Use Activism as a Form of Self-Care

It's not always easy to stay centered in the face of discrimination and sexism. Taking breaks from the media can also be challenging, especially since it seems like there's a new story about racial injustice daily. As much as it's important to take breaks, you are also more than welcome to take healthy action against injustices. Social activism can be used as a form of self-care. It can allow you to express your concerns about issues that impact you alongside people with the same experiences. Taking care of yourself doesn't involve denying your reality, so it's natural to take action. It's also common for the things that stress you out to continue to affect the healed or healing version of you.

Getting trapped in despair happens when you aren't accepting the things you can't control. So, some moments require you to sit back and let what is be what it is. Feeling upset or wanting to stand up for yourself is also healthy. If there are moments that present themselves for you to rise and take action, you also don't need to feel bad about it. You want to think about what you can do to get yourself away from feelings of hopelessness. You are not powerless, and at times, taking action is a reminder of how powerful you are. For instance, you can take action by joining a group centered around racial justice to push transformative change in lawful ways. Permitting yourself to connect with a collective of activists who share similar ideologies and strive for the same things as you can be inspiring. It can remind you that you are far more capable of being an agent of change than you know. Connecting with a group of people who share your values can build your circle and help you learn, heal, and grow in more ways than you can imagine.

Plus, being around a group of like-minded people can increase joy. It can also show you different ways to enjoy life and take pride in being a Black woman. In group settings that honor your identity, you get to be happy in your skin without justification.

Take Care of Your Mental Health

Almost 30% of young people within the Black community say they don't receive the mental health assistance they need (Fleming, n.d.-b). The experiences of racial violence that flood the internet—every way our Black brothers and sisters are harmed—can be detrimental to emotional health. It's also just highly triggering to see how little the world cares about Black people.

However, just because the world undermines your greatness doesn't mean you should join in. Start appreciating yourself and taking care of your mind to stand against discrimination, heartache, and other experiences that come with your greatness. It's essential to care for your mental health, especially as a Black woman. The following tips can help you protect and nurture your mental health.

Regulate What You Watch

It's okay and important to be picky about your social media and news intake. The things you watch and read contribute significantly to how you think, feel, and process things. Since your mental health is on the line, it's good to regulate what you watch. Know which content adds to your life and what doesn't. Choosing to avoid things that could trigger racial trauma isn't selfish. You can support racial activism without subjecting yourself to emotional torment from watching challenging situations. Your mission should be to remain healthy and sharp, which you can do by regulating your media intake.

Be Attentive to Your Feelings

Notice how certain situations and interactions make you feel. Strong emotions don't just disappear because you deny them, so embracing your feelings is important. Not being attentive to your feelings is like suppressing the inner child or telling her that she is meant to be "seen, not heard." It's a way of retraumatizing yourself. Yet, listening and being attentive to your feelings is also a way of healing yourself. You get to practice self-compassion. Doing so prevents aggression, outrage, and emotional outbursts.

Also, being attentive to your feelings is self-protection and care. When you are repeatedly exposed to trauma, that sense of care and protection is removed; emotional attentiveness helps you regain it. Attentiveness to your feelings helps you find a healthy outlet, such as journaling, talking to someone, or relaxing with a long cry.

There's no expectation for how you should deal with trauma, and individual processes are different. That's why being attentive to your feelings is essential. It can help you identify what you need, so you can handle your healing journey in a manner that suits you best. Not only is your vulnerability okay, but recognizing it also helps you process life meaningfully. Attentiveness to your feelings enables you to move through them gracefully—supporting yourself as you would a friend. Allow yourself to feel whatever the emotion is without criticism, which inspires major transformation and emotional regulation.

Take Breaks From Social Media

It can be tempting to read or watch content when it's easily accessible, even when you know how harmful it is. For example, those videos showing yet another Black man being treated inhumanely are damaging. Yet, they are also all over the internet. It's not healthy to be exposed to such cruel and unnatural treatment of Black people. So, taking breaks from social media to avoid seeing those things can benefit your mental health immensely.

Separate yourself from your television, computer, and phone for a while. Just taking several hours to yourself can be more refreshing than you know. Your body and mind need a reset now and again. Sleep is your body's way of resting, while taking a break from social media can be your mind's way of disconnecting from the havoc in the world. A mental reset like this allows you to refocus on what matters to you.

Choosing to take social media breaks is significant protection against mental health conditions. However, for someone who might not have the option of a break, changing your social media settings could help. For example, if you work in the social media space, then leaving the platforms might not be an option. Instead, blocking sensitive content online and on other media platforms could be more realistic. Doing so will ensure you manage what you see and don't see. On Instagram, X, Facebook, and many other platforms, there are settings available to protect yourself against receiving unwanted information. Using those settings could be a great substitute for someone without the option to take breaks from social media.

Find a Physical Outlet

While it's not always easy to stay on top of good mental health practices, it's important. Finding a physical outlet usually helps you to escape the internal turmoil and avoid being caught up in your head. Some beneficial physical outlets to clear your head include walking, doing a dance routine, stretching, getting into yoga, and many more enjoyable things. The goal of any activity is to give you a break from emotional processing and reduce the stress caused by trauma.

Manage Difficult Thoughts in Safer Ways

Trauma causes rumination—the continuous overload of harmful or unpleasant thoughts. These can cause you to lose self-confidence and lean toward risky coping mechanisms. Due to racial trauma, you might find yourself battling to stop negative thoughts from flooding in, particularly when you are in predominantly White spaces. Your mind could work over time with overwhelming thoughts of what people think, how they perceive you, and so many other anxieties. You might even struggle to stop flashbacks of videos you watched from playing in a loop in your head. Whatever your experience is, ruminating adversely affects how you live your life moving forward.

If you notice your trauma impacting your sleep and eating patterns, it is an early sign of distress. Other warning signs that trauma is impacting your life include

- feeling anxious

- feeling afraid

- irritability

- feeling upset

- persistent feelings of sadness

- prolonged and intense self-doubt

- unexplained moodiness

These difficulties can feel overwhelming and act as a sign that trauma is impacting you profoundly. Battling these symptoms is normal, but getting help as soon as you notice them is crucial. Of course, it's always great to seek assistance much before these symptoms worsen or hit the surface.

Managing complex thoughts in safer ways can save and transform your life. You can do this by using this book's interactive elements and the complimentary workbook. Relaxation techniques, understanding your trauma, embracing your history, identity affirmation, mindfulness, and all the other strategies from the previous chapters are helpful tools for managing rumination.

Equally, starting a conversation with someone you trust about needing help is beneficial. This can be a close friend, a trusted parent, or an older family member. Your siblings or a coach, teacher, mentor, mental health professional, or spiritual leader are also valid options. It doesn't matter who you reach out to as long as it's someone you trust with the information you need to share. Also, this person needs to have the emotional capacity to handle what you have to share and be willing to take on the heaviness of your feelings. Sometimes, the people close to you could be going through similar difficulties and find it hard to stand in the gap for you in this way. Fortunately, that's where professional advice comes in.

Seek Professional Help

Everyone struggles sometimes; it's a part of the human experience. Also, everyone deserves help with what they are working with. Seeking professional help through therapy or qualified counsel can help you healthily navigate challenging times. Mental health care can come in many forms, from personal therapy sessions to family time and group settings.

Maybe, you need to talk to someone about something specifically related to managing the relationship issues caused by trauma, and a coach in this field could help. Or perhaps, you're struggling with a mental condition that causes suicidal thoughts or significant depression, and a psychiatrist could be the best route for you. Regardless of your feelings or how overwhelming you believe your experiences are, you don't have to manage things in isolation. Help is always available for you; reach out and receive it. You'll notice how much better you get at dealing with adversity and addressing future issues. Learning the necessary coping mechanisms pushes you toward a more fulfilling, joyful future.

Opening up to someone with the professional obligation to help you sort through your thoughts and emotions is highly helpful. The benefits of this are broad, but the primary advantage is that a professional can help you see your problems from a more objective perspective. This is the best way to find effective tools for healing and overcoming these challenges.

If you are interested in getting help on a professional level, feel free to research groups or individual therapists that offer the support you need. Groups help you find comfort and belonging in sharing experiences with people with similar feelings. Individual therapy, on the other hand, offers you the privacy and confidentiality you need to get things off your chest without judgment. Both can be helpful.

No matter which healthy route you take to find help, remember to do what's best for you. Your mental health is important, and getting help ensures that you stay cared for in that regard. Assessing your emotions, owning your feelings, and taking steps toward transformation are how you can manage the effects of trauma.

Support Social Justice Without Hurting Your Mental Health

Sitting on the sidelines as injustice plays out can make you feel guilty or enraged, which isn't good for your healing either. If you believe you should be a part of the change and charge against racial discrepancies, it's okay. However, there's a way to support social justice without damaging your mental health. As we discussed earlier, you need to set some rules around your social media consumption. Then, start appreciating yourself and taking care of your mind to stand against discrimination, heartache, and other experiences that come with your greatness.

Taking care of your mental health by doing what's best for yourself isn't selfish. This is the foundation for how you will continue supporting others on their racial trauma healing journey. When you aren't okay, you can't help anyone else. Now, once you've started the work on yourself and feel you can handle social support, you can start doing things to show solidarity without retraumatizing yourself and others.

Share the Life, Not the Trauma

One of the first things you can do is to share the lives of the people who have been brutally affected by racial trauma. Show your love by celebrating theirs. Too often, the media circulates images of Black people in pain, being violated, or as criminals. Yet, plenty more images and stories of Black success, joy, healing, contribution, and positivity are being swept under the rug. You can be a part of the change that people need to see. Start sharing more of the life that needs to be celebrated rather than reposting the violence.

Instead of focusing on the brutality of how someone was treated or harmed, choose to share the beauty of their life. Doing so humanizes them in the face of injustice. It gets others to see how beautiful and vibrant Black people can be. Also, it shows us living lives beyond violence and trauma; that's where the power is.

Instead of repeating the violent issues, talk about the memory and positive things that people contribute. This is how you support social justice issues without falling into the trap of retraumatization. You become part of the collective rewrite as you help Black lives be recognized as meaningful and purposeful rather than in the light of victimhood. Use your social media to spread the good; it will do wonders for your health and others.

Take Peaceful, Lawful Action

Protesting peacefully with people who share a similar outlook to you provides a supportive sense of community and a healthy outlet for anger at racial injustice. Taking peaceful, lawful action promotes unity and helps you feel a part of something bigger than yourself. Collective protesting can also make you feel like you are serving your community, which can be encouraging. You can participate in organizations such as the NAACP, Black Voters Matter, and many more.

Don't Neglect Your Needs

There could be mounting pressure to react or stand up for social justice daily, but you may not have the emotional bandwidth some days. It's vital to avoid living in survival mode, whereby you deplete all your capacity trying to stand in the gap for your community. Not neglecting your needs looks like taking a step back to breathe and process when you need it. You have your entire life to continue social justice practices, so taking breaks occasionally is healthy.

Introduce Humor Into Your Daily Experiences

Humor builds resilience and brings happiness into tough situations. Smiling and laughing daily prompts the brain to release endorphins (hormones that regulate mood) to get you back to a good place. Some benefits of humor include positive changes in body chemistry, increased human connection, and higher resilience.

Humor is helpful when it enhances your experiences and brings you joy. However, it's counterproductive when it's used to hide or deny how you feel. At no point should you use humor as deflection because it's important to embrace your emotions. If you aren't confident about how you use humor, here are some questions that you can ask yourself:

- Do I joke about things that are still painful to me?

- Am I using humor as a defense mechanism?

- Is my humor appropriate to the situation?

- Does my humor bring a connection or remove me from it?

You can introduce more humor into your life through productive entertainment and observations. This can include watching funny videos, doing something silly, reading funny material, and getting into comedy.

Celebrate Being a Black Woman

Enjoying and claiming your identity as a Black woman is a form of self-care. As a young Black woman, celebrating yourself creates a sense of pride about your multifaceted identity. It helps you connect to your sense of self and your communities, which can act as a buffer against the impacts of racial prejudice and discrimination.

You can celebrate being a Black woman by

- supporting Black businesses.

- sharing in your culture.

- visiting museums that celebrate Black work.

- immersing yourself in experiences of Black joy.

- creating new traditions.

- finding people you relate to.

- reciting affirmations

Being Black is phenomenal. It would help if you affirmed that within yourself. Lean into the beauty of being a part of the Black community. Enjoy your rich culture and diversity. Acknowledging the joy and beauty of being Black is incredibly beneficial to your mental health.

Conclusion

The strong Black woman narrative is based on our ancestors' resilience and ability to overcome the worst racial environments. Today, Black women don't have to just be strong. Young Black women can be soft, loved, affirmed, and given the safe space to be human—just like everyone else. There's no shame in embracing your humanity and vulnerabilities. Your openness and desire to live life from a more positive lens isn't a weakness but a strength in itself.

Once you've unpacked what trauma is to you and the effects it has on your life you can start to use the tools listed in the book to alleviate its impact. For example, seeking professional help; spending time with people who understand your experiences; investing in your mental and physical health; taking breaks from social media; and supporting social justice without compromising your health can all help you live an authentic, joyful life.

Resist the urge to be victimized by the world and live from a place of self-pity because there's no power there. Your empowerment is in choosing to heal from rough experiences and defy racial trauma by noticing and celebrating your joy. Get in touch with your inner child, and let her tell you what she needs. Living beyond your trauma is about honoring your needs in the face of difficulties. You are in the best position to care for yourself, and the tools in this book are resources to help you.

Choosing to be more than your trauma isn't about denying your history or the present circumstances that perpetuate it. Instead, it's about recognizing that you don't have to submit to discrimination or injustice. You can live a life that's bold, happy, and free—one that acknowledges that being a Black woman isn't synonymous with pain, victimhood, and trauma. There's more to being a Black woman than the scars you've carried until now; there's joy, purpose, and beauty. Affirming your identity in this way will build your confidence in who you are. It will also make you a valuable contributor to the world around you. Keeping a positive outlook on your life and what you are capable of makes it more possible to be part of significant change, and that's the goal.

The world needs more people who are invested in healing and becoming the best version of themselves. So, don't let microaggressions and racial discrimination rattle you and cause you to focus on the shadow of your existence when there is, in fact, so much light. Choose to turn your face toward the hope and beauty of your being rather than continue harmful narratives linked to your identity. Engaging with this book's complementary workbook can also help you reach your transformation goals as you continue to grow and become more self-aware. You have all it takes to be the joyful, most healed version of yourself as a Black woman. Hopefully, you feel encouraged to implement this book's healing lessons in your life.

Thank you for taking this journey. If you found value in these words, please consider leaving a review. It helps other readers as well the authors.

Author Biography

Victoria Anderson is an emerging voice in the field of self-discovery and empowerment, celebrated for her unique perspective on healing from childhood trauma and defying societal expectations. Her story is deeply intertwined with her own experiences of overcoming obstacles that sought to limit her potential. Growing up in a vibrant yet challenging urban setting, Victoria encountered societal stereotypes that attempted to confine her dreams. However, her unwavering determination to break free from these constraints led her to pursue education as a means of transcending boundaries.

After graduating from a prominent university, Victoria embarked on a personal quest to understand the complexities of childhood trauma and societal pressures. Motivated by her struggles and the stories of individuals she encountered, she devoted herself to extensive research and introspection, seeking ways to facilitate healing and personal growth. Victoria's writing reflects her deep understanding of the human experience, infused with empathy and wisdom. Through her work, she aims to guide others toward self-discovery and overcoming adversity, offering insights and strategies for navigating life's challenges.

As a passionate advocate for mental health and personal development, Victoria extends her impact beyond her writing. She engages in speaking engagements, captivating audiences with her authentic storytelling and empowering messages. Additionally, she actively participates in community outreach programs, mentoring and supporting young people as they navigate their paths toward resilience and empowerment.

Victoria Anderson's commitment to fostering healing, reshaping perspectives, and nurturing resilience serves as an inspiration to those grappling with childhood trauma and societal pressures. Her dedication to igniting transformation and instilling hope continues to influence and uplift individuals on their journeys of self-discovery.

References

A closer look at freeze, the third stress response. (n.d.). Ashley Addiction Treatment. https://www.ashleytreatment.org/rehab-blog/learning-about-stress-responses/

Acupuncture. (n.d.). Johns Hopkins. https://www.hopkinsmedicine.org/health/wellness-and-prevention/acupuncture

Africans in colonial America. (n.d.). National Geographic. https://education.nationalgeographic.org/resource/africans-colonial-america/

Anxiety and panic attacks. (2021, February). Mind. https://www.mind.org.uk/information-support/types-of-mental-health-problems/anxiety-and-panic-attacks/panic-attacks/

Asare, J. G. (2022, February 14). *3 Ways intergenerational trauma still impacts the black community today.* Forbes. https://www.forbes.com/sites/janicegassam/2022/02/14/3-ways-intergenerational-trauma-still-impacts-the-black-community-today/?sh=531975c33cf6

Bachert, A. (2023, April 18). *The flop trauma response.* Charlie Health. https://www.charliehealth.com/post/flop-trauma-response

Bowdler, J. (2023, September 14). *What is caregiver trauma?* Primecarers. https://primecarers.co.uk/providing-care/caregivers/what-is-caregiver-trauma

Bradley, C. (2019, January 2). *A meditation for exploring your senses.* Mindful. https://www.mindful.org/a-meditation-for-exploring-your-senses/

Brady, A. (2016, March 31). *6 Tips to master your internal dialogue.* Chopra. https://chopra.com/blogs/meditation/6-tips-to-master-your-internal-dialogue

Bryant, A. (2019, March 14). *Change your inner dialogue.* Self Leadership. https://www.selfleadership.com/blog/change-inner-dialogue

Bryant, T. S. (2023, April 1). *Column: Trauma: Surviving, healing, and thriving.* American Psychological Association. https://www.apa.org/monitor/2023/04/surviving-trauma

Burnett-Zeigler, I. (2022). *The other side of the strong black woman.* Northwestern Magazine. https://magazine.northwestern.edu/voices/inger-burnett-zeigler-the-other-side-of-the-strong-black-woman/

Carter, C. M. (2023, February 6). *Examples of institutional racism: What it is and what you can do.* Health. https://www.health.com/mind-body/health-diversity-inclusion/institutional-racism

Carter, L. K. (2019). *Do you really see me? Understanding trauma in African American women.* Health. https://health.maryland.gov/bha/suicideprevention/D ocuments/Behavioral%20Health%20Symposium%202 020/2E-%20Do%20You%20Really%20See%20Me_%20Unders tanding%20Trauma%20in%20African%20American%2 0Women%20(Abb).pdf

Castelin, S., & White, G. (2022). "I'm a strong independent black woman": The strong black woman schema and mental health in college-aged black women. *Psychology of Women Quarterly*. https://doi.org/10.1177_03616843211067501

CBC Radio. (2022, February 25). *Why I refuse to call myself a "strong black woman."* CBC. https://www.cbc.ca/radio/docproject/why-i-refuse-to-call-myself-a-strong-black-woman-1.6365370

Childhood trauma and its effect on healthy development. (2012, July). National Center Brief. https://edn.ne.gov/cms/sites/default/files/u1/pdf/se14Childhood%20Trauma%20%26%20Its%20Effect%20on%20Healthy%20Development.pdf

Cook, B. (2021, October 19). *How reparenting your inner child can create emotional healing and integration in your life.* Medium. https://medium.com/know-thyself-heal-thyself/how-reparenting-your-inner-child-can-create-emotional-healing-and-integration-in-your-life-4b68863e3044

Cooks-Cambell, A. (2023, November 28). *Triggered? Learn what emotional triggers are and how to deal with them.* BetterUp. https://www.betterup.com/blog/triggers

Cooks-Campbell, A. (2022, March 15). *How inner child work enables healing and playful discovery.* BetterUp. https://www.betterup.com/blog/inner-child-work

Cozier, Y. (2022, February 24). *POV: What "strong black woman" means to me.* Boston University. https://www.bu.edu/articles/2022/pov-what-strong-black-woman-means-to-me/

Deering, S. (2023, May 19). *How 'doomscrolling' impacts your mental health—and how to stop.* Verywellmind. https://www.verywellmind.com/what-is-doomscrolling-5088882

Dforsythe. (2017, July 31). *Black women and PTSD: How do you know if you have it?* Black Women's Health Imperative. https://bwhi.org/2017/07/31/black-women-ptsd-know-ptsd/

Different types of microaggressions. (n.d.). EasyLlama. https://www.easyllama.com/chapter/different-types-of-microaggressions/

Dissociation and dissociative disorders. (2023, January). Mind. https://www.mind.org.uk/information-support/types-of-mental-health-problems/dissociation-and-dissociative-disorders/about-dissociation/

Dixon, E. (2021, July 3). *Breaking the chains of generational trauma.* Psychology Today. https://www.psychologytoday.com/za/blog/the-flourishing-family/202107/breaking-the-chains-generational-trauma

Donovan, J. (n.d.). *Self-care and recovery after trauma.* WebMD. https://www.webmd.com/mental-health/ss/slideshow-emotional-trauma-self-care

Drevitch, G. (2023, November 26). *12 Questions to help recognize childhood trauma.* Psychology Today. https://www.psychologytoday.com/za/blog/invisible-bruises/202311/a-12-question-test-for-childhood-family-trauma

Ferguson, S. (2019, February 20). *PTSD causes: Why people experience PTSD.* Healthline. https://www.healthline.com/health/mental-health/ptsd-causes#treatment

Fight or flight response. (n.d.). Psychologytools. https://www.psychologytools.com/resource/fight-or-flight-response/

Fleming, L. (n.d.-a). *How to break free of the 'Strong Black Woman' stereotype.* The Jed Foundation. https://jedfoundation.org/resource/how-to-break-free-of-the-strong-black-woman-stereotype/

Fleming, L. (n.d.-b). *How black youth can take care of their mental health after racial violence.* The Jed Foundation. https://jedfoundation.org/resource/how-black-youth-can-take-care-of-their-mental-health-after-racial-violence/

Fleming, L. (n.d.-c). *Using humor as a healthy coping mechanism.* The Jed Foundation. https://jedfoundation.org/resource/using-humor-as-a-healthy-coping-mechanism/

Fletcher, J. (2023, November 14). *How to validate yourself.* PsychCentral. https://psychcentral.com/health/ways-to-validate-yourself

Gardner, A. (2022, July 28). *17 Symptoms of PTSD everyone should know.* Health. https://www.health.com/condition/ptsd/ptsd-symptoms

Gillespie, C. (2023, August 11). *What is generational tauma?* Health. https://www.health.com/condition/ptsd/generational-trauma

Gillette, H. (2023, April 4). *Trauma-related disorders: More than PTSD.* Healthline. https://www.healthline.com/health/mental-health/trauma-related-disorders#types

Godbolt, D., Opara, I., & Amutah-Onukagha, N. (2022). Strong black women: Linking stereotypes, stress, and overeating among a sample of black female college students. *Journal of Black Studies, 53*(6), 609. https://doi.org/10.1177/00219347221087453

Goldstein, E. (n.d.). *What is an inner child & what does it know?* Integrative Psychotherapy. https://integrativepsych.co/new-blog/what-is-an-inner-child

Goldstein, I. (2023, March 31). *Why inner child work is having a moment & how to try it, from therapists.* MBGmindfulness. https://www.mindbodygreen.com/articles/how-inner-child-work-became-so-popular

Gupta, S. (2023, November 16). *What is trauma therapy?* Verywellmind. https://www.verywellmind.com/trauma-therapy-definition-types-techniques-and-efficacy-5191413

Herman, J. L. (1998). Recovery from psychological trauma. *Psychiatry and Clinical Neurosciences, 52*(1), S98-S103. https://doi.org/10.1046/j.1440-1819.1998.0520s5S145.x

Heyl, J. C. (2023, March 22). *Inner child work: How your past shapes your present.* Verywellmind. https://www.verywellmind.com/inner-child-work-how-your-past-shapes-your-present-7152929#citation-1

The health benefits of tai chi. (2022, May 24). Harvard Health Publishing. https://www.health.harvard.edu/staying-healthy/the-health-benefits-of-tai-chi

Halland, K. (2019). *Understanding age regression.* Healthline. https://www.healthline.com/health/mental-health/age-regression#is-it-safe

Hollowell, A. M. (2019, June 14). *The cost of being a "strong black woman."* Depaul University. https://via.library.depaul.edu/cgi/viewcontent.cgi?artic le=1317&context=csh_etd

How to cope with sleep problems. (2020, May). Mind. https://www.mind.org.uk/information-support/types-of-mental-health-problems/sleep-problems/about-sleep-and-mental-health/

How drugs and alcohol can affect your mental health. (2022, June). Mind. https://www.mind.org.uk/information-support/types-of-mental-health-problems/recreational-drugs-alcohol-and-addiction/how-drugs-and-alcohol-can-affect-your-mental-health/

Hylton, K. (2017). I'm not joking! The strategic use of humour in stories of racism. *Ethnicities.* https://doi.org/10.1177/1468796817743998

The importance of routines. (2020, January 2). Fort Behavioral Health. https://www.fortbehavioral.com/addiction-recovery-blog/the-importance-of-routines/

Jones, M.K., Harris, K.J. & Reynolds, A.A. (2021). In their own words: The meaning of the strong black woman schema among black U.S. *Springer Link.* 84, 347–359. https://doi.org/10.1007/s11199-020-01170-w

Khoddam, R. (2022, March 31). *Breath and trauma-healing exercises.* Psychology Today. https://www.psychologytoday.com/za/blog/the-addiction-connection/202203/breath-and-trauma-healing-exercises

King-White, D. (2022, June 8). *Intergenerational trauma: What it is & how to heal.* Choosing Therapy. https://www.choosingtherapy.com/intergenerational-trauma/

Kivi, R. (2018, September 29). *Acute stress disorder.* Healthline. https://www.healthline.com/health/acute-stress-disorder#risk-factors

Krouse, L. (n.d.). *How you can cope with racism and racial trauma.* The Jed Foundation. https://jedfoundation.org/resource/how-you-can-cope-with-racism-and-racial-trauma/

Lawrence, T. E. (n.d.). *Celebrating your black identity is self-care.* The Jed Foundation. https://jedfoundation.org/resource/celebrating-your-black-identity-is-self-care/

Lebow, H. I. (2021, June 3). *Can you recover from trauma? 5 Therapy options.* PsychCentral. https://psychcentral.com/health/trauma-therapy#best-therapy-for-trauma

Leonard, J. (2020, June 3). *What is trauma? What to know.* Medical News Today. https://www.medicalnewstoday.com/articles/trauma

Li, P. (2024, January 11). *7 Tips to breaking the generational trauma cycle.* Parenting for Brain. https://www.parentingforbrain.com/trauma-cycle/

Lockett, E. (2023, September 28). *What do microaggressions look like in healthcare? Here are some examples.* Healthline. https://www.healthline.com/health/microaggression-examples-in-healthcare

Lovering, C. (2022, February 28). *7 Relaxation techniques for effective stress and anxiety relief.* PsychCentral. https://psychcentral.com/lib/relaxation-exercises-and-techniques#for-anxiety-relief

Majors, D. (2023, July 15). *Leadership affirmations for a black woman.* LinkedIn. https://www.linkedin.com/pulse/leadership-affirmations-black-woman-dovie-majors-mba-coss

Malcolm X: 'The most disrespected person in America, is the black woman', Speech to women - 1964. (n.d.). Speakola. https://speakola.com/political/malcolm-x-speech-to-black-women-1962

Manke, K. (2019, December 5). *How thee "strong black woman" identity both helps and hurts.* Greater Good Magazine. https://greatergood.berkeley.edu/article/item/how_the_strong_black_woman_identity_both_helps_and_hurts

Marie, S. (2021, December 23). *What are the best types of therapy for trauma?* PsychCentral. https://psychcentral.com/health/best-types-of-therapy-for-trauma

Martin, S. (2019, November 15). *Why it's so important to validate yourself and how to start.* PsychCentral. https://psychcentral.com/blog/imperfect/2019/11/why-its-so-important-to-validate-yourself-and-how-to-start

Meditation: A simple, fast way to reduce stress. (2023, December 14). Mayo Clinic Staff. *Mayo Clinic.* https://www.mayoclinic.org/tests-procedures/meditation/in-depth/meditation/art-20045858

Miller, D. A. (2023, May 18). *African American women make meaning of historical trauma.* The University of San Francisco. https://repository.usfca.edu/cgi/viewcontent.cgi?articl e=1636&context=diss

Misachi, J. (2019, December 12). *List Of African American Museums.* WorldAtlas. https://www.worldatlas.com/articles/list-of-african-american-museums.html

Post-traumatic stress disorder (PTSD). (2021, January). Mind. https://www.mind.org.uk/information-support/types-of-mental-health-problems/post-traumatic-stress-disorder-ptsd-and-complex-ptsd/symptoms/#Flashbacks

Quinn, D. (2023, July 27). *Generational trauma: 13+ effective ways to break the cycle.* Sandstone Care. https://www.sandstonecare.com/blog/generational-trauma/

A quote from Audre Lorde. (n.d.). https://www.goodreads.com/quotes/437563-caring-for-myself-is-not-self-indulgence-it-is-self-preservation-and

Racism and mental health. (n.d.). Mind. https://www.mind.org.uk/information-support/tips-for-everyday-living/racism-and-mental-health/#RacialTrauma

Raypole, C. (2024, January 26). *How attachment disorders impact your relationships.* Healthline. https://www.healthline.com/health/attachment-disorder-in-adults

Raypole, C. (2023a, March 27). *9 Tips to help you kick off your self-discovery journey.* Healthline. https://www.healthline.com/health/self-discovery#visualize

Raypole, C. (2023b, February 13). *8 Ways to start healing your inner child.* Healthline. https://www.healthline.com/health/mental-health/inner-child-healing

Raypole, C. (2022, February 8). *How many thoughts do you have each day? And other things to think about.* Healthline. https://www.healthline.com/health/how-many-thoughts-per-day

Raypole, C. (2020, September 1). *Positive affirmations: Too good to be true?* Healthline. https://www.healthline.com/health/mental-health/do-affirmations-work

Relaxation techniques: Try these steps to lower stress. (2024, January 24). Mayo Clinic Staff. *Mayo Clinic.* https://www.mayoclinic.org/healthy-lifestyle/stress-management/in-depth/relaxation-technique/art-20045368

Reparenting yourself and why it's important. (n.d.). Integrative Psychotherapy. https://integrativepsych.co/new-blog/heal-inner-child-counseling-five-towns-nassau

Resnick, A. (2023, November 9). *How to heal from trauma.* Verywellmind. https://www.verywellmind.com/10-ways-to-heal-from-trauma-5206940

Robinson, L., Smith, M., & Segal, J. (n.d.). *Emotional and psychological trauma.* Help Guide. https://www.helpguide.org/articles/ptsd-trauma/coping-with-emotional-and-psychological-trauma.htm

Ryder, G. (2022, January 10). *The fawn response: How trauma can lead to people-pleasing.* PsychCentral. https://psychcentral.com/health/fawn-response

Ryder, G., & White, T. (2022, April 15). *How intergenerational trauma impacts families.* PsychCentral. https://psychcentral.com/lib/how-intergenerational-trauma-impacts-families#who-it-affects

Satiating the need for emotional connection. (n.d.). Integrative Psychotherapy. https://integrativepsych.co/new-blog/relationship-counseling-five-towns-nassau

Scott, E. (2020, June 25). *Use guided imagery for relaxation.* Verywellmind. https://www.verywellmind.com/use-guided-imagery-for-relaxation-3144606

Self-harm. (2020, May). Mind. https://www.mind.org.uk/information-support/types-of-mental-health-problems/self-harm/about-self-harm/

76 Healing trauma quotes and affirmations + free printable affirmation cards. The Wellness Society. https://thewellnesssociety.org/76-healing-cptsd-quotes-and-affirmations/

Shange, N. (2022, August 11). *Opinion: Disrupting the harmful 'strong black woman' narrative.* UFS. https://www.ufs.ac.za/templates/news-archive/campus-news/2022/august/opinion-disrupting-the-harmful-strong-black-woman-narrative

60 Affirmations every black woman needs to hear. (2021, September 11). Balanced Black Girl. https://www.balancedblackgirl.com/10-affirmations-guide-glow-up/

Star, K. (2023, January 3). *The mental health benefits of physical exercise.* Verywellmind. https://www.verywellmind.com/mental-health-benefits-of-exercise-2584094

Taylor, M. (n.d.). *What does fight, flight, freeze, fawn mean?* WebMD. https://www.webmd.com/mental-health/what-does-fight-flight-freeze-fawn-mean

Trauma. (n.d.-a). American Psychological Association. https://www.apa.org/topics/trauma

Trauma. (n.d.-b). Psychology Today. https://www.psychologytoday.com/za/basics/trauma

Trauma. (2023, December). Mind. https://www.mind.org.uk/information-support/types-of-mental-health-problems/trauma/about-trauma/

Trauma and violence. (n.d.). SAMHSA. https://www.samhsa.gov/trauma-violence

Trieu, T. (2023, April 10). What Is Inner Child Work? A Guide To Healing Your Inner Child. MBGmindfulness. https://www.mindbodygreen.com/articles/inner-child-work

Understanding mental health triggers. (n.d.). Campus Health. https://campushealth.unc.edu/health-topic/understanding-mental-health-triggers/

Using affirmations. (n.d.). Mind Tools Content Team. *Mindtools.* https://www.mindtools.com/air49f4/using-affirmations

Webb, J. (2022, March 31). *Why strong black women need mental health care.* Health Evolution. https://www.healthevolution.com/insider/why-strong-black-women-need-mental-health-care-too/

What are microaggressions? (2022, February 1). Cleveland Clinic. https://health.clevelandclinic.org/what-are-microaggressions-and-examples

What is box breathing? (2023, April 30). WebMD Editorial Contributors. *WebMD.* https://www.webmd.com/balance/what-is-box-breathing

White, C. N. (2021). *When being strong hurts: Trauma and the strong black woman stereotype.* University of California. https://scholarcommons.sc.edu/cgi/viewcontent.cgi?article=7289&context=etd

Wilding, M. (2021, August 9). *8 Easy tricks to quiet negative inner dialogue.* Psychology Today. https://www.psychologytoday.com/za/blog/trust-yourself/202108/8-easy-tricks-quiet-negative-inner-dialogue

Wisner, W. (2023, January 26). *25 positive daily affirmations to recite for your mental health.* Verywellmind. https://www.verywellmind.com/positive-daily-affirmations-7097067

Women of color in the United States (quick take). (2023, February 1). Catalyst. https://www.catalyst.org/research/women-of-color-in-the-united-states/

Woods-Giscombe, C., Robinson, M. N., Carthon, D., Devane-Johnson, S., & Corbie-Smith, G. (2015). Superwoman schema, stigma, spirituality, and culturally sensitive providers: Factors influencing African American women's use of mental health services. *Journal of Best Practices in Health Professions Diversity : Research, Education and Policy*, *9*(1), 1124. https://www.ncbi.nlm.nih.gov/pmc/articles/PMC7544 187/

Yehuda, R., & Lehrner, A. (2018). Intergenerational transmission of trauma effects: Putative role of epigenetic mechanisms. *World Psychiatry*, *17*(3), 243-257. https://doi.org/10.1002/wps.20568

Yu-Hsin Liao, K., Wei, M., & Yin, M. (2019). The Misunderstood Schema of the Strong Black Woman: Exploring Its Mental Health Consequences and Coping Responses Among African American Women. *Psychology of Women Quarterly*. https://doi.org/10.1177/0361684319883198

www.ingramcontent.com/pod-product-compliance
Lightning Source LLC
Chambersburg PA
CBHW070806280326
41934CB00012B/3076